MY
TIME
WILL
COME

MY
TIME
WILL
COME

A MEMOIR OF CRIME, PUNISHMENT, HOPE, AND REDEMPTION

Ian Manuel
Foreword by Bryan Stevenson

RANDOM HOUSE
LARGE PRINT

Published in the United States of America by
Random House Large Print in association with Pantheon
Books, a division of Penguin Random House LLC,
New York, and distributed in Canada by
Penguin Random House Canada Limited, Toronto.

Cover design by Linda Huang, based on an original image
by Glenn Paul for the Equal Justice Initiative.

The Library of Congress has established a
Cataloging-in-Publication record for this title.

ISBN: 978-0-593-39652-0

www.penguinrandomhouse.com/large-print-format-books

FIRST LARGE PRINT EDITION

Printed in the United States of America

10 9 8 7 6 5 4 3 2 1

This Large Print edition published in accord with
the standards of the N.A.V.H.

I dedicate this book to Linda Johnson,
for loving me unconditionally.

To Peggye Manuel for giving me life.
All I needed was a chance.

To Debbie Baigrie for forgiving me.

To Bryan Stevenson for my freedom.

And to all of those who told me that
I'd never amount to anything, that
I'd die nameless, just another number
in prison, I hope my story helps you
believe in miracles and magic. It was
you, the naysayers, who gave me the
motivation to seek the impossible,
to keep clinging to the faith in my
darkest hours, to know that My Time
Will Come . . .

Foreword by Bryan Stevenson

WHEN I FIRST MET IAN MANUEL IN A Florida prison, he was not allowed to be in the same room with me. As an attorney meeting a client, I could have a contact visit with almost any other prisoner at the facility but that would not be possible with Ian because he was barred from direct contact with other people. He would have to be on the other side of a thick glass wall in a separate room; we would have to talk through a tiny hole. In preparing for the visit, Ian and I had both hoped that prison officials would relent and allow a proper visit but that request was repeatedly denied.

They brought Ian into his glassed room restrained in a chained outfit I'd never seen before. He was bound in a jumpsuit made of heavy-duty nylon that opened from the back but was padlocked at the neck and waist. It was a full-body straitjacket that so confined his ability to move that he couldn't walk, he had to waddle from side to side. I'd had hundreds of contact visits with death row prisoners before my meeting with Ian but this was new to me. It took me a while to get over the spectacle of such violent restraints on such a young person inside a secure facility.

Ian and I had exchanged several letters and spoken on the phone many times before we met. Our calls were sometimes emotional because Ian was trying to understand what was happening around him or what he was experiencing, I often heard pain and anguish in his voice. I would frequently tell Ian I was proud of him and he told me later that this sometimes confused him.

At our first visit, Ian told me he was nervous about meeting in person. I asked him why and he said he didn't want to disappoint me. I tried to reassure him but he said he was still nervous. Then he told me he'd written a poem he wanted to recite, so I, of course, said I would listen. It was at that peculiar moment in our first meeting, in that unforgiving, cold prison, that Ian, constricted and absurdly bound with chains and restraints, spoke his poetic words. His poem spoke about grief and sadness, strength and resolve, and most important, hope and love. His words tried to make sense of things that were overwhelming and complex. His poem was about his existence and what he seemed to provoke in the people around him; it was a lament for freedom and forgiveness. I was very moved by his words. I told Ian that his poem was beautiful and he smiled. It's the smile that I remember most about our first meeting.

It is cruel to say to a child of thirteen that you are so beyond hope or redemption, your life is so irredeemable and without value, that you must die in prison. What we've done to children in this country—condemning them and throwing them away—is shameful. Ian Manuel is one of thousands of kids who have been sentenced to life imprisonment without parole for crimes they were accused of when they were children.

Ian's conviction was followed by torturous imprisonment. He was too small to be housed in general population at the adult prison where he was sent, so they placed him in solitary confinement for nearly two decades. His abusive isolation was justified by misguided protocols and a devastating lack of understanding about adolescent development, mental health, or behavioral science. What happened to Ian is beyond cruel but sadly not unique. We have traumatized tens of thousands of unaided children who have been incarcerated in adult prisons for decades; we still do it today.

I'd read Ian's file and it was clear he was being abused and abusing himself and others in response. But, at our first visit, he still managed to recite his poetry. Despite the humiliating and degrading cloak of bondage he was forced to wear, you could still see resolve and compassion in his eyes.

I left the prison with great hope for Ian.

Children are magical. Nothing in the human experience affirms the gift of life, the beauty of our existence more than our children. Infants have an extraordinary ability to make the most hardened of us feel inexplicably joyful when they smile. Small children have a curiosity and capacity for affection and love that can uplift, move, and transform us. So much of what we do in life is organized around protecting, caring for, and loving our children.

But we don't all mean the same thing when we say "our children." For some, that's a much more specific and narrow universe. For me, "all children" are "our children," but after representing hundreds of kids in jails and prisons, I've come to realize that's not everyone's view.

Americans have long embraced the priority that children represent which makes the story of Ian Manuel so critically important and simultaneously hard to understand. We've done something terrible in this country to a generation of our children, something we've yet to fully acknowledge or address. Our poorest and most vulnerable children—those born into extreme poverty, violent neighborhoods, or violent families, those in greatest need of assistance have largely been abandoned in many communities.

Hundreds of thousands of children in this country live in spaces where they are neglected, abused, and mistreated. They are forced to grow up without consistent love and affection, without safety, without guidance or direction. Many of these children suffer from trauma disorders by the time they're five years old.

Any human being will be traumatized if they are subjected to constant danger, shouting, anger, and violence that causes fear. Our brains begin to produce cortisol and adrenaline when we are threatened or stressed. When we're constantly menaced, our brains overproduce these chemicals, flooding our bodies with stress hormones even when there is no immediate threat. Like the thousands of combat veterans whose symptoms led to greater attention to post-traumatic stress disorders, thousands of American children develop trauma disorders before they start school. Of course, these toddlers and young children never signed up for violent combat and their plight has received far less attention.

We have done very little to help these children. In fact, when these kids go to school we aggravate their condition by threatening them. We tell many vulnerable children they'll be suspended or expelled if they don't behave like healthy kids with no trauma or disabilities. We deny these young people critically urgent mental health care and too often, we deprive them of safety, which is the most effective treatment for children coping with trauma.

Many of our children get worse and develop all kinds of problems. Some children try to manage the feeling of always being imperiled by using drugs or seeking unhealthy stimulation or dangerous escape. Some kids join gangs to feel less alone in their struggle to survive. We harshly punish traumatized children for making these kinds of choices even though extreme punishment just makes things worse. Most judges, prosecutors, lawyers, and advocates fundamentally misperceive the nature of the problem—and as a result, they repeatedly make decisions that add to the burden of our most vulnerable kids. This brutal system is part of Ian Manuel's story.

There are serious consequences when we fail to respond effectively to extreme poverty and the abusive and unhealthy living conditions found in rural and urban communities across this country. Children suffer, engage in dangerous behaviors that undermine health and safety, and lives are lost.

We live in a nation that has failed to prevent guns from being placed in the hands of traumatized, unsupervised thirteen-year-old children. That, of course, inevitably leads to tragedy. Debbie Baigrie became a tragic shooting victim as a result of Ian's struggles. His painful story reveals a cycle of dysfunction and neglect that exposes our flawed system and our collective failure to help people with great needs. But Ian's story is also inspiring; a story of hope that should compel us to recognize we can and should do better.

It turns out that Debbie Baigrie is an extraordinary human being. She is remarkably strong, compassionate, and thoughtful. She forgave Ian and became his ally and champion.

It turns out that Ian is also extraordinary despite his violent act. He searches for beauty and purpose in the midst of great suffering. He struggles against certain death in an obscure prison cell mandated by the courts to win freedom. Both Debbie and Ian have made powerful statements to the world.

Debbie Baigrie has said to the world that there should be nothing "ordinary" about thirteen-year-old children shooting adults and that we need to do extraordinary things to help address the horrific problems in American society that allow child trauma and violence to be so poorly managed.

Ian is now able to say to the world that it should never be "ordinary" or acceptable to condemn a child to die in prison. Through his remarkable spirit and resolve, he has survived a cycle of abuse and violence, a saga of tragedy and dysfunction and still held on to his humanity.

Ian is magic. His story is difficult and heartbreaking, but he takes us places we need to go to understand why we must do better. He survives by relying on a poetic spirit, an unrelenting desire to succeed, to recover, and to love. Ian's story says something hopeful about our future.

We remain the nation with the highest rate of incarceration in the world. We have condemned thousands of children to die in prison who are still incarcerated today. Our prison system is notoriously cruel, and we have shown a shameful unwillingness to help the most needy, disabled, and traumatized people in our nation. But, Ian's story affirms that we can turn things around. His journey reminds us that we are, in fact, more than the worst thing we've ever done.

I used to tell Ian I was proud of him not because he was succeeding in prison or even because he was gifted and talented. I was proud of him for believing he was more than a crime despite what everyone around him said. I was proud of Ian for refusing to surrender his humanity in the face of horrific, inhumane conditions of confinement. I am proud, because as this book dramatically illustrates, Ian has held on to his magic.

MY
TIME
WILL
COME

1

MY STORY HAS BEEN TOLD MANY TIMES. You can read it in police files and court records, case notes and daily logs. The story of my birth, for example, told by a judge sentencing my mother to prison soon after my arrival in this world. And there's the story of that day when I was five, in the case notes of a social worker who drove me to a foster home and then, a few days later, drove me back to the projects, to the room I had shared with my abuser. The story of my childhood was told multiple times by juvenile probation officers who found me to be a problem best managed inside the walls of institutions. In the illustrious space—cold and intensely bright in my memory—of an adult courtroom, it would be the robed and sober voice of a judge who would foretell my death when I was thirteen. Relying on the stories of police officers, lawyers, and other accomplished professionals, he would send me to Florida State Prison, never to be released. As I said, my story has been told many times and by highly regarded experts in their fields. But today, if you'll bear with me, I would like to try to tell it to you myself. I have reason to believe the experts may be wrong about me. You see, today, thirty years later, I am neither in prison nor dead.

In the stories told of my life, each begins with a crime. A crime by my mother against a neighbor, crimes against me, crimes committed by me. My stories are defined by legal codes and diagnostic categories. To tell you the truth, I struggle to shake these, to describe myself to you as I am, in all that I am. My sense, though, is that this is an experience true to millions of people who, like me, happened to be born into poor neighborhoods at a time in history when the intervention of choice is arrest and incarceration—even for mothers of infants, even for young children. I would like not to begin my story as the experts have done, with the story of a crime. But that is, in fact, the reality of this life. So I will begin with the story of the worst thing I have ever done, the crime I was sentenced to die in prison for. But I begin here not because, as the experts have said, this defines me. I begin here because I hurt someone very badly during a time in my life when I was blinded by my own hurt. And I want to admit to it. I want to state the truth of it. I think I owe it to her. And to the child that I was. I think we need to speak about harm, what we've done, what's been done to us, because that is what will open doors, what will air out and begin to heal the wounds we carry and have caused. And that is what will allow for new stories to begin to be told. I am telling you my story today because I want to tell a story of hope and meaning, of being one among a human family.

I SHOT DEBBIE BAIGRIE ON JULY 27, 1990. I was thirteen and, along with a group of older boys, I was trying to rob her and the man who was walking her to her car. He, of course, was walking her to her car out of concern for her being a woman, alone at night, in a parking lot. My friends and I were the embodiment of his reasons for concern and I believe that night I only confirmed any beliefs he had about kids like me.

At the time, my mom and I were homeless, staying with a family friend in the housing projects I had called home most of my life. Central Park Village had been a prosperous, entrepreneurial black community before I was born. But after deadly riots and looting there in 1967, the neighborhood had fallen on hard times. It was now a complex of run-down, low-rise buildings, riddled with poverty, gang violence, drugs, and crime. Because Mom had let the rent on our place fall behind, she and I were staying with a lady known to me as Aunt Louise, though she was no relation of ours. During my childhood, Central Park Village was a place of comings and goings, among family, friends, and acquaintances; the place was full of people like us—roamers.

GUNS WERE NOT NEW TO ME. WHEN I WAS eleven, my friend Marquis and I had gone jacking, committing our first crimes together—robbing people, seventy-five cents here, two dollars there—only to be arrested. The gun we had brandished turned out to be an old, rusty, empty Colt M1911, the standard-issue sidearm of the U.S. Armed Forces from 1911 to 1986. Toward the end of that school year, during a conflict I had with a classmate, Marquis's cousin had pulled the gun out, pointed it at my opponent, and insisted that I fight him. The gun I would end up using to shoot Debbie was a .32 revolver.

On the night of the crime, I met up with Marquis, who was fourteen at the time, and two older boys from the neighborhood and we walked downtown. Downtown Tampa was my stomping ground for a couple of years. I knew where police cars were stationed; where it was too crowded to pull off a robbery; where it would be unlikely for us to get caught.

We continued downtown, searching for the right place at the right time, but I was nervous.

Marquis was stern in a friendly way: "Man, Jim-Jim, look it done turned nighttime and we ain't done nothing yet. The next people we come across, we jacking, whether it's too open or not." Everybody agreed. We didn't have far to go before an opportunity presented itself: as we were walking across the parking lot, we turned to see a white man and woman, leaning against a car, rapt in conversation.

One of the boys cooked up a plan on the spot. "Jim-Jim, I'm gonna go over and ask 'em for some change. When you see one o' dem reach for dey money, do your thing." "All right," I said. Marquis and the other boy stood right behind me. "Do one of y'all have change for a twenty?" the boy asked. I thought I heard either the man or the woman say yes. At the top of my lungs I yelled, "It's a jack, y'all, give it up," pointing the revolver at them. The woman stared at the gun and screamed, which startled me. Before I knew it I had pulled the trigger and she took off, running.

TAKE IT BACK

Her mouth opens as she inhales her
    scream.
The bullets are reloaded because the
    trigger was never squeezed.
We're back at the start when we first
    asked for change.
And her face is the same because she
    never felt that pain.
He isn't on his knees—looking me in
    my eyes.
Like I'm the last thing he'll see for the
    first and final time.
The song self-destruction isn't
    resounding in my mind.
We're just standing at the scene.
    Before it became a crime.
If I could see into the future. Sitting
    on that porch on India.
When my codefendants came to visit.
    I'd've chosen to stay with Lydia.
I'm back in Central Park. Two-story
    apartment building.
Never knowing where I'm going . . .

I stared down the man and barked, "Get on the fucking ground." He stood motionless, terrified. Ever so slowly the man got on his knees. For a moment I stood trembling, shaken to the core. As the woman ran I aimed the gun at her fleeing figure, and squeezed the trigger. She screamed but kept running, disappearing around the corner.

I turned back and started sprinting toward Central Park. The other three boys running behind me, I could hear Marquis say, "Jim-Jim, hold up, man, hold up, wait for me, don't leave me here." When I asked the three "How much y'all get?" Marquis answered, "He ain't have nothin' on him, Jim-Jim, nothin'."

THAT NIGHT, CENTRAL PARK VILLAGE WAS abuzz with rumor and gossip about what had happened. People I had known all my life in the neighborhood—people who had given me rank and praise for jacking in the past—were now clearly intent on keeping their distance from me.

"No, boy, get away from me. I heard what you did downtown."

"Say what?"

"Man, Marquis told us you just killed two people downtown."

A police car pulled up on State Street and called me over.

"You been in the park all night?"

"Yeah, why?"

"Because you fit the description of somebody who took part in a shooting downtown today. A woman was shot."

I couldn't be seen downtown wearing the Bulls shirt that had matched the description of a young black shooter on the loose. I turned to a little boy on a bicycle. He was a few years younger than me, about eight or nine. He had been sitting on his bike with one foot on the curb quietly watching us.

"Lil Cal, trade shirts with me until I come back." He had on a gray and blue Georgetown Hoya T-shirt. Without hesitation, he said, "Here you go," and began pulling the shirt over his head.

I WAS BORN MARCH 29, 1977, IN TAMPA General Hospital to Peggye McClendon Manuel. When as a child I asked her why she named me Ian Einar Manuel (Ian being

Scottish Gaelic for God's gift; Einar, Old Norse for lone warrior), she told me it was pure serendipity: she claimed to have pulled Ian and Einar out of a bag of names. "If your sorry-ass daddy would've showed up at the hospital and signed your birth papers, you would've had his no-good-ass name (Jimmy Reese, Jr.). He told me he was going to get some Pampers and milk; I ain't seen him since." I would learn much later that Ian is a variant of Sean, the name of my older brother. As to Manuel, after divorcing my brother's dad, Robert Manuel, Peggye had kept his name.

Soon after I was born, my mother was sent to a prison for shooting a woman with a .32 revolver. As the story goes, Sean, known as "John-John," had taken to wandering through the woman's yard and she had sternly reprimanded him, prompting my mother to warn her that she had better leave Sean alone, that is, if she knew what was good for her. Now the woman had gone so far as to slap my brother, who ran home and told our mother. Enraged, Peggye pulled her gun from its hiding place, walked over to the woman's property, and shot her at point-blank range but didn't kill her.

After Peggye was arrested, her best friend, Lynn Creal, whom we called "Aunt" Lynn, borrowed money from a neighborhood loan shark, Joe Upshaw, to bail her out of jail. When it was time for my mother to be sentenced, she grew angry: "I'm here for protecting my son. If you gon' send me to jail for that, then go right ahead . . . I don't give a damn."

Judge Coe didn't either. He sentenced her to three years.

With Mom in prison, I was shunted to and fro among Peggye's friends, who did the best they could to take care of me. But it was my paternal grandmother, Linda Johnson, who conclusively stepped up. She constantly worried Lynn, begging her to let her look after me until my mother was released. Lynn ended up taking me to visit my mom at Lowell Correctional Institution. "Ian's grandmother won't leave me alone about this boy," she told Peggye. "I can't take no more! I'm going to give him to her till you come home."

· · ·

GRANDMA LINDA WAS BORN IN DECEMBER
sometime between 1911 and 1920. She was
raised in Cordele, Georgia. She bore two
children, a daughter and a son. In search of
a livelihood, my grandmother had migrated
to Tampa, forced to leave both of her children behind. She found work as a cook in
Morrison's Cafeteria at the Tampa Bay mall.
She would hold that job for more than
twenty-five years before retiring. I recall little
of my infancy spent with Grandma Linda,
but I have the dearest memories of her from
age six on, years after my mother's release
from Lowell. While Peggye could express her
love only in sometimes hard-to-fathom ways,
my grandmother adored and spoiled me as
only a grandparent can.

The first of every month, Grandma would
receive a social security check, a retirement
check, and free food coupons from Morrison's,
and she'd say in her singular southern drawl,
"Come on, boy, we're going out yonder."
"Out yonder" was the Tampa Bay mall.

We'd walk downtown and sit on a bench
to wait for the Hartline bus. When it pulled
up—the orange, yellow, and red Hartline

strip painted along its sides—its doors would swoosh open, inviting us in. Grandma Linda would give the bus driver two quarters and two dimes to pay our bus fare, thirty-five cents each for the trip to "out yonder." The bus would roll away from downtown along Main Street, through west Tampa, past Macfarlane Park, toward Tampa Bay mall. I always eagerly anticipated passing, and staring through the window at, the Old Sombrero—Tampa Stadium. The bus would eventually roll into the parking lot and stop at the mall's entrance.

Sometimes we'd walk past Morrison's Cafeteria as we stepped through the mall's glass entrance to go cash Grandma Linda's checks. At other times we'd head straight for the cafeteria. I still remember my usual haul there: fried shrimp, mac and cheese, sweet potato pie, and sweet tea. Grandma never ate much herself.

After our meal, if we still had to go to the bank, we'd walk up to the counter, and Grandma would take out her checks and give them to the teller. Then I'd wait for my inevitable embarrassment when the teller would turn the checks over and say, "Just sign right here, Mrs. Johnson, and we'll get you your money." Grandma would always have to say, "I don't know how to spell my name!"

The teller always responded: "It's OK, ma'am, just put an X and that'll be good enough."

With relief, I'd exhale and watch Grandma carefully mark her two Xs; the teller would count out and give her her money, between eight and nine hundred dollars, which to my mind meant that she was rich. Before returning home from "out yonder," Grandma Linda would often load me up with goodies—toys, clothes, shoes, sweets, whatever I wanted.

IF I TOLD MY STORY

If I told my story . . .
Would you believe a word I said?
Or would the truth be like a
   square root—
too deep and difficult to understand.
If I told my story . . .
And all the times I've bled.
How I played hopscotch, over
   blood drops.
A result of a childhood, curtailed in
   a cell.
If I told my story . . . of the water—
splashing closed eyelids like a dam.
One million tears that never spilled.
A wounded heart just waiting
   to heal.
If I told my story . . . of courage.
And my will to act in spite of
   my fears.
How I survived being buried alive—
You probably wouldn't believe
   your ears.

**If I told my story . . . of guts
    and glory.
Without sugarcoating the facts.
It would be obvious, without much
    argument.
That I've lived a miraculous life.**

. . .

LATER, THE NIGHT OF THE SHOOTING, ALL hell broke loose at the Hall in Central Park Village, the game room. To get there, you had to step through a hole in a wall, a passageway through a blockade of brick and concrete that was big enough for a man to go through. When I found myself standing on the other side in a sandy area, I saw two Central Park kids rounding a corner, running from the game room. They were carrying a bounty of candy and other sweets, which struck me as odd, because the game room was closed at night. I yelled, "What y'all doing?"

"Jim-Jim, we just broke in the Hall," they excitedly replied.

I walked around the corner to the front of the Hall and pushed the door open.

Word must have spread swiftly. The press of the crowd was intense. Pure mayhem. Men with crowbars were busting up the videogame machine for quarters. Women were arguing over cases of cigarettes and food. People were running back and forth, in and out the door, hauling cases of beer and jars of pickles.

Behind the counter I saw a big pig's feet jar full of pennies. I grabbed it and ran.

No sooner had I stepped through the hole in the wall headed back to Central Park than I heard the all-too-familiar sound of police sirens, the cars pulling in off Nebraska Ave. toward the Hall. I took off as fast I could, the heavy jar of pennies slowing me down.

After the police left, I was standing on State Street and saw Tammy, a girl I knew who was pregnant with the baby of legendary Tampa fighter Frank "Baldy" Green. I looked at Tammy's bulging stomach and thought of a way to give her the pennies.

"Tammy," I said, "I'm a give you these pennies, but after you have that baby, I want to hold that baby as many times as there are pennies in this jar."

Tammy smiled brightly and said, "OK, Jim-Jim."

BUYING TIME

If I could buy time
I'd pay for the past
Reach into the glass
And pick memories out of the sand
I'd spend money on moments
I was interacting and laughing
Subtract loneliness and sadness
Then add up the balance.
I'd watch how I spend it
Because time is precious.
Be very selective
And buy times I was happy.
If time could be purchased
I'd bring back my family
Roll back all of the hearses
And open their caskets.
I'd alter results
Because I'd know what would happen
And would feel it's my fault
If I just sit back and let it
I'd break a bill
And ask for change
So this time things

Wouldn't turn out the same.
If I could buy time
I'd pay for some smiles
Recreate all of the days
They've destroyed as a child
If time could be bought
I'd purchase moments I lost
Every tick tock on the clock
No matter how much it cost.

. . .

"WHEN THE NURSE CLEANED YOU UP AND brought you to me, I said, 'That ain't my baby; I don't know what y'all did with my baby. You better take this black mother-fucker back where you got him from and bring me my child.'" For as long as I can remember, after her release from prison, my mother often recounted this. Often absent, she had a mean streak. All the same, my love for her was stubborn, even though her capacity for cruelty ended up damaging me in ways that I'm still trying to figure out. When I misbehaved, she would whip me with an extension cord or switch, but her words hurt even more. Insults flew from her mouth like bullets.

"Jim-Jim, you make me sick. The more I teach you, the dumber I get," or "You ain't my son, I found you on the doorstep." Sometimes, she compared me to a neighborhood boy named Corey. "I wish you had been cute like Corey. That was a beautiful baby." Once she told me, "Ian, go outside and play." I went and looked out the window, only to see that there were no other children around. "There's nobody outside to play with." "Jim-Jim, you came out of my pussy by yourself. If God wanted you to have somebody to play with, I would've had twins."

Peggye McClendon Manuel was born in Belle Glade, Florida, the gateway to the Everglades, a wild and rough place near Lake Okeechobee, where a lot of migrant workers gathered before fanning out all over the state, following crops that needed picking. She didn't stay in Belle Glade long. She and her brother, George, were taken from their mother and sent to live with her mother's sister and husband in Orlando when she was a little girl because her mother, my grandma Betty, was a single parent and an alcoholic. I don't know if my mother ever knew her father. She lived with her aunt and uncle until she finished middle school, when she started fighting with her uncle. After one fight too many, when she was around fourteen, she was sent alone to Tampa to rejoin her mother, who had married the man I knew as Grandpa Sonny. Peggye made it clear to me from an early age that I was unwanted, a mistake. When she became pregnant with me, my brother, Sean, was nine years old, and the last thing she wanted was another child to feed and clothe. I remember asking her once if I could have a sister, to which she responded: "I ain't having no more damn kids. You better ask your sorry-ass daddy to have you a sister. Your black ass ain't supposed to be here, let alone a sister. If I would've followed my first mind and got an abortion instead of listening to Big Momma, Ian Manuel wouldn't exist." Big Momma—at least five foot ten and more than three hundred pounds—was the neighborhood matriarch, whose proclamations were definitive.

My mother hated the darkness of my skin so much that, as a child, I wished I were of lighter complexion. There was a time when I had heard that chlorine could change pigmentation, so I'd sit in the shallows of the neighborhood pool (I couldn't swim) and repeatedly submerge my body. When I'd get out of the pool, I'd purposely ignore the lifeguard yelling, "Boy, wash that chlorine off of you." Later, when I was eight or nine, I started taking bleach baths. I'd get Clorox from the basement laundry room and walk back up the twelve concrete steps. I'd stop the tub up, turn the hot water on, and wait for the tub to fill. I would always have to decide how much bleach to pour in—not because I feared damage to my skin but because I worried that my mother would beat me for using up her bleach. Sometimes I would risk as much as half a bottle. If the water was too hot, I'd adjust the temperature by briefly turning on the cold water faucet. Slowly I'd sink into the tub and slide down to my neck, sometimes losing track of time as I soaked. In my child's imagination, I was trying to achieve the color of a son that my mother would be proud of and love.

STRETCH MY IMAGINATION

If I could stretch my imagination
and split my thoughts apart—
I'd reach past our separation.
And pull you closer to my heart
If I could stretch my imagination
I'd disintegrate these bars.
Reach upwards with my arms.
Until my fingers touched
   the stars.
If I could stretch my imagination.
like the muscles in my legs.
I'd be the chest where you rest.
Every time you're scared.
If I could stretch my imagination
like a thousand rubber bands.
I'd pull the strings of your heart
until they popped me on
   my hands.
If I could stretch my imagination.
like a rainbow in the clouds.
I'd navigate icebergs and
   glaciers.
For the radiance of your smile.

If I could stretch my imagination.
And bend the stiffness of my mind.
I'd see past my limitations
Until I could stare into your eyes.
If I could stretch my imagination. . . .

. . .

WHEN I WAS FIVE, MY MOTHER, BROTHER—
Sean Pierre Devon Manuel—and I lived
in a two-bedroom apartment in Central
Park Village, a family of three on Burden
Court—at once all too aptly and ironically
named. If I had a family portrait of the three
of us at the time, one glance at it would make
you think we weren't related. I was the runt
of the family. I didn't really start to grow until
about the sixth grade, and I never got to be
more than five feet, ten inches. Peggye was
a big woman, but short. She weighed more
than 220 pounds and was only five foot two.
Sean was a giant next to both of us. He was
always tall for his age, and by the time he
was sixteen, was more than six feet tall and
about 230 pounds. On my birthdays, I would
sometimes put on his forty-two-inch-waist
pants to see how much I'd grown. They always swallowed me as easily as a whale might
swallow a minnow. Sean, "John-John," was
my idol. He was an excellent fighter and well
respected, not just in our neighborhood but
in others throughout Tampa. I was proud to
be Lil Jim-Jim, John-John's little brother. I

wanted to be as big and bad and respected as John-John.

When my mother was home, she liked to sit on a brown wooden dining room chair on the porch next to the front door. She always had a yellow box of Argo cornstarch, her snack of choice, and a clear tumbler filled with RC cola and ice cubes. She'd finish her RC and then crunch and suck the ice cubes, before lighting up a Winston 100s cigarette. When she was not at home, she more than likely could be found at Momma Dump's, near our project. The actual name of the bar was Blue Light, but it belonged to Momma Dump, so that's what everyone called it. There, Peggye drank beer after beer.

The front door of the bar was propped open by a chair most of the time, unless it was too cold or rainy. Inside, to the left of the front door, was a jukebox and to the right a phone booth. Straight ahead were a couple of green pool tables. The bar was at an angle to the left. It wasn't that long; it had only five or six barstools. Aside from the expected kaleidoscopic panorama of bottles of liquor on the shelves, there were jars of pig's feet and pickles as well as boxes of candy. Even though we kids weren't supposed to be there, occasionally I would wander in looking for my mother, and sometimes Momma Dump would hand me some candy and say, "Now, Jim-Jim, you know you're not supposed to be in here. Get on out of here before I lose my license."

IT WAS DURING THAT TIME THAT JOHN-John sexually abused me. While the details are sparse in my mind—for self-protective reasons, no doubt—I remember enough to know I didn't need or want to remember any more. Mine was a painful initiation into sex and the streets' supposed sacred code of silence. When he would finish he would tell me, "Don't tell Momma! Understand?" And I would nod yes. Little as I was, I was full of shame and fear; I didn't break the code of silence for a long time. But one day Peggye and I were downstairs in the dining room of our apartment. Sean wasn't there. Momma and I were getting ready to leave for an outing. While tucking my shirt into my unbuttoned pants, my mother said, "Boy, where your drawers at?" I stood frozen, speechless, in a daze. I couldn't think of a lie fast enough. Louder, she repeated the question. Her mother's intuition must have told her something was terribly wrong. I began crying. Now she knew something was grossly amiss. She grabbed me by the shoulders: "What happened? Tell me! Tell me!" Through tears, my voice cracking, I said, "John-John."

My mother buttoned me up, got on the phone, and called the police. The police came and interviewed my mother and me; they arrested my brother. Child welfare services spirited me off to a shelter home; they temporarily took custody away from my mother as they conducted their investigation.

Even in the home of concerned, friendly white people, I was in shock at being separated from my family. I had a nightmare my first night at my new foster parents' home. I woke up screaming my dead "uncle's" name, "Bobby! Bobby!" I was comforted by unfamiliar faces. Sean was sent to a juvenile facility for six months or so. After he came out, we returned to our life together, John-John and I back in our old bedroom. It was never spoken of again.

TWO DAYS AFTER THE SHOOTING, I WENT downtown and retraced the woman's steps as she had frantically run from the crime scene—from the car that she had been leaning on while talking to the man to the corner where she had turned. On the sidewalk around the corner I spotted what I took to be dried drops of blood. For the first time it dawned on me that I had actually shot someone. I remember it was a hot afternoon and the sun was in my eyes. Maybe it had been a while since I had eaten. But I walked into a fire station and told them I thought I needed help, shortly before fainting. I woke up in the hospital to my mother yelling at the nurses.

As I would later learn, I had shot Debbie Baigrie, a twenty-eight-year-old mother of two girls, in the face. She had survived.

2

I DON'T KNOW HOW TO SWIM AND I'M scared to death of deep water. The night after the shooting, I dreamt I was thrashing about at sea to avoid drowning. I slept worse than fitfully. Time and again I woke up anxious, terrified. I was full of regret, though remorse for what I had done would come later. The next morning I went to work, as I did on occasional weekends, for Bob Gilbertson at the Tampa Young Men's Christian Association—as close to a father as I have ever known.

My biological father had been a blur in my life. He cropped up sporadically when least expected. Jimmy Reese was a hardworking trucker for the Fogarty Brothers; he drove a green and white truck. As a young man he had earned the nickname "Rock Jaw" for a reason lost to time. My very first memory of him is of a drunk stumbling into his mother's—Grandma Linda's—house to watch wrestling on TV, around the time my brother molested me. On another occasion there, annoyed by my behavior, he tried to beat me. Grandma Linda would have none of it and chased him out: "Don't you hit my baby; you drunk, get out." Two or three times a year, he would come around to my mother's house, I assume to give her a little something to help take care of me. His idea of fatherly time was to say to her: "Lemme get that boy for a little bit." And he would take me to the outskirts of Central Park Village, where he lived, toward Tampa Heights, to places like the 8-Ball, a bar where older men hung out and gambled. It had videogames. Or he would say to my mom: "Lemme get that boy for the weekend." And I would have to go spend time with him and his girlfriend, Beverly. He would babble to me about inconsequential matters like a man with a guilty conscience. He would dole out pocket change as if to buy my affection. He once bought me a boom box, which I ended up selling or pawning. I didn't need a boom box. He told a story about me, when I was between ages one and four, which still haunts me: he, Beverly, and I were in a house. They were asleep; I was not. The house caught fire. I must have woke to the smell of smoke. I crawled, screaming, waking them up. My father said I had saved all of our lives.

IAN-GREDIENTS

Sprinkle seasons of solitude
in a crockpot of confinement.
Chop the hottest jalapenos
and rub'em in the wounds of
    your body.
Burn family members like tinder
that died in the 2000s and '90s.
Choke down hard times past
    your larynx
like a toddler swallowing solids.
Open bottles of ketchup
from the tomatoes beneath
    your pigments.
Turn up the gas behind the glass
and let'em bake you like a biscuit.
Or sleep inside a freezer
with nothing but your skin.
Then fidget inside a mixer
as they beat you like an egg!
Then you'll begin to understand
how difficult my life has really been
and the ingredients that it took
Make me everything I am.

. . .

WHEN I WAS SIX, GRANDMA LINDA learned that her daughter, my aunt, had died. Grandma Linda packed a suitcase and she and I headed downtown to the Greyhound station to catch a bus for Cordele, Georgia, to attend the funeral. This was my first and only visit to my grandmother's birthplace. Cordele was a rural, predominantly black and desperately poor town in southern Georgia, inhabited by the descendants of sharecroppers, in a region known as the Black Belt. We stayed with my cousin Isadora, a sweet, young brown-skinned woman. I remember meeting my cousin, Ken, only a few years older than I was. He took me out in the house's backyard, where the family had pigs locked in a pen and rabbits in a cage. He showed me how to feed the animals. I stood in stunned amazement as he poured two buckets of slop into the pen; the pigs rushed toward it, greedily slurping, and devoured it. Later, we went to the church for the funeral. I watched as they lowered my aunt's casket into the ground, Grandma Linda holding my hand.

Soon after Grandma Linda and I returned

home to Tampa, we were standing at a bus stop where she was seeing me off to school as she did every morning. I don't remember what brought things to a head, but Grandma Linda started yelling at me in front of the other kids waiting for the bus. I yelled back. She slapped me hard across the face. I slapped her back, knocking her down. I blurted, "Grandma, I'm sorry." As she rose to her feet, she said, "Come on. I'm taking you to your momma." I began to cry and beg: "Please, Grandma, don't tell Momma. I'm sorry."

When she told my mom, I was ordered to my room and I was certain I was about to get the beating of my life. But, instead, I heard Momma blame Grandma for what had happened. "You treat that boy like a king. Buying him this and that, everything he asks for. Stop and I bet he'll straighten up." I heard Grandma Linda say, "I is," in a small voice. I think back now on all of the humiliation my grandmother faced as she struggled to pull herself and her children—and now her grandchild—out of poverty, all of the courage it took to travel as a young black woman from Cordele to this city, so different from what she knew. It is a sharp wound in my heart to remember how I treated her in that moment, how I hurt the person I loved most in the world, who loved me and made love possible for me even now.

LINDA'S LOVE

I want a woman that can hold me—
like the little boy I am.
The one incarcerated as a kid.
And forced to be a man.
A lady that will cradle me—
arms around my head.
As I cry for the little boy—
the world just left for dead.
I want to be loved for who I am—
particularly the darkness of my skin.
Because I've been abused
    and ridiculed—
for something I had no choice
    in being.
I want a woman to be that
    something—
I haven't had since Grandma Linda.
To be my partner, and my pillow.
A place I can just surrender.
Someone who treats me special—
like Grandma did when I was a kid.
Someone I can trust, take off
    the mask.

Relax and just be Ian.
Maybe I'm just a dreamer.
Asking for the impossible.
Somebody to love me devoutly—
A woman like Linda Johnson.

.   .   .

GRANDMA LINDA LIVED ACROSS THE STREET
from the St. Peter Claver Elementary School.
She paid for my tuition to attend, starting in
first grade, and for the next two and one-half
years, sat on her front porch each day, watching me like a hawk through the schoolyard's
fence when I was at recess.

St. Peter Claver's school was established
in 1893 to serve children of the black community. It was soon destroyed by fire; the
notice tacked on an oak tree in front of the
ruins read: "the late fire on these grounds was
not caused by any ill feeling to the Catholic
Church, but because the citizens do not pro-
pose to submit to a negro school in the midst
of the white and retired resident portion of
the city." Despite threats of violence, it was
rebuilt by brave black men and women determined to educate their children, in a setting
of prayer, worship, and learning. At St. Peter
Claver when I went, little black children were
resplendent in crisp uniforms: girls in long-
sleeved white shirts under dark blue tartan
pinafores, and boys in short-sleeved light blue
or white shirts and dark blue pants. Thanks to

my grandmother, it was here that I developed a love for school, especially for the care and devotion of teachers whose praise I craved.

At the end of the school year awards were handed out in the auditorium where proud parents sat with their children. As the ceremony neared its conclusion—kid after kid had been called to the stage—I began to fear embarrassment next to my mother and her friend Linda Wright. Finally, Mrs. Yvonne Fort, a middle-aged black teacher, called my name: "And to Ian Manuel for excellence in reading and writing." I walked up, beaming, accepted my certificates, and thanked Mrs. Fort. When I returned to my seat Mrs. Wright said in a hushed voice: "Jim-Jim, lemme look at those certificates. Reading and writing, baby, that's all you need in this world. As long as you've got that, you can be anything you wanna be."

There was also the issue of the Eucharist. I remember sitting mesmerized by the rite as I watched Father O'Keefe refer to the communion bread and cup of wine as the actual body and blood of Christ. "Jesus said, 'Do this in remembrance of me.'" Father O'Keefe then fed the little white discs to the children who stepped up to the altar, each accompanied by his or her parent. I was excluded from the sacrament. When I mustered the courage to ask a teacher why, she told me that only kids with parents in tow could participate. After school that day, I joyously hurried home.

"Momma, listen, I need you to come to my school's church with me next week."

"For what?"

"Well, they gave kids this thing to eat today and I asked why I couldn't get none and they said my parent had to be there."

"Boy, I ain't going down there for that shit. That ain't nothing but some damn bread. If you want some bread, drag your ass into the kitchen and get it."

Grandma Linda developed dementia over the next few years. I remember when she could no longer control her bowels. Her embarrassment and confusion—and my own. Isadora came one day to take Grandma Linda back to Cordele, where she would be placed in a nursing home for the remainder of her days. I would never see her again. I'm not even sure when she died. It is hard to even begin to estimate this loss for me. It was as if, at eleven years old, it was time for me to grow up—no one to care if or what I ate, no one to walk me to and from the bus, no one to wonder where I was or what I was doing or with whom. It was at this moment that I first understood what it meant to be homeless, to be without anything to hold me in place and offer shelter and comfort—and was pulled fully into the chaos of Central Park Village.

In the middle of the school year, I would have to start attending my district's public school, Morgan Woods Elementary, located in the Tampa upper-middle-class suburb of Town and Country, a twenty- to thirty-minute bus ride from Central Park Village via the interstate highway—twice as big as St. Peter Claver and consistently ranked among the lowest performing public schools in Florida.

IN CENTRAL PARK VILLAGE, THE ONLY OP-tions for an eleven-year-old boy like me to earn real money were to mug people or become a drug runner for the major players in the 'hood. I wanted no part of that, regardless of how much I had glamorized my brother, Sean, who at this point in my life was serving time behind bars. I decided with my friend Ron that we would just head downtown and secure gainful employment. I don't know why but I was confident that if I could get somebody to listen to me, I would be able to convince them to give us jobs. "Who's gonna give us a job? We're kids," Ron objected. I told him to let me do the talking.

After a few fruitless encounters, we ended up at the YMCA beneath the monorail to Harbour Island, a mall built along the Hillsborough River. I said to the lady at the front desk, "Me and my friend are looking for a job; do you have an application that we can fill out?" She looked at us amused, obviously finding our bravado cute. "You'll have to speak to Sandy, my manager, over there." Sandy ran the YMCA gym. "Sir," I began and repeated what I had said to the woman. "Why don't you go next door to the administrative office and see if they have anything for you?" he responded. I was fierce in my determination. Once she knew why we were there, Bob Gilbertson's secretary walked into his office and returned to say that her boss was busy but that we should wait. Soon we were ushered in and found ourselves standing before Mr. Gilbertson, CEO of the YMCA, who had ultimate authority to hire us—he was an affable, clean shaven (except for a mustache) white man about six feet even, weighing more than two hundred pounds, and of business casual style.

"Where are you guys from?"

"Central Park Village; we're looking for something to keep us off the streets, to help us with school clothes and things like that, you know, to support ourselves a little bit."

"Well, what can you do?" he asked as we all sat down.

"Clean windows, wipe down the exercise bikes, sweep."

"Gosh, guys, I can't very well give you a job, but I'll tell you what, I'll buy you lunch and then let's talk."

Bob gave us a twenty-dollar bill and directed us to a pizza joint up the street. He told us to come back with the change, which we did. Unbeknownst to us then—but as we would later learn—Bob knew as much about

Central Park Village as anybody. He was aware of the poverty and danger permeating the 'hood. He understood how lack of hope could shatter lives, and how Central Park was toxic to children, forced as they were from an early age to conform to the unforgiving code of the streets, where respect is earned by never allowing oneself to be dissed without consequence. The more he had learned about Central Park, the more he had wanted to connect with it and nurture the potential of its children and teenagers, but logistics had posed a problem: the nearest Y with youth programs was in the suburbs. Years later, after exhaustive fundraising, Bob was able to build a YMCA branch closer to the projects. For me, what stood out about Bob when I first met him was that he didn't treat me like a child; he didn't blow me off. He saw something of value in an eleven-year-old boy who had had the courage—the courage, I like to think, of my Grandma Linda—to walk into his office and ask for work.

To be sure, Bob could never have put us on the Y's payroll, which I didn't know at the time; there are child labor laws after all.

We chatted about what might be possible—
maybe summer camp one day—and unex-
pectedly Bob proposed that we do odd jobs
around his house for pay. From the start,
Bob was always challenging us: "Ian, if you
saved one penny and doubled your savings
every day, how much money would you have
in ten years?" Bob was always talking about
the importance of budgeting. He lived in a
world apart from Central Park Village, in the
prosperous area near Bayshore Boulevard in
Tampa, with its elegant houses, freshly cut
grass, and nice cars. Going there for me was
both pleasurable and disorienting; it inspired
me to dream but also to worry about whether
I could or would ever truly live in Bob's world.
When word got out in Central Park that Ron
and I had "jobs," other kids wanted in, and
eventually two other boys our age, Jose and
Donte, ended up joining us.

Soon we settled on a routine: many a
Saturday our group went out to Bob's house
to perform chores such as trimming hedges
and weeding the yard. Afterward Bob would
take us to lunch in the neighborhood. We
would then do fun things, for he treated us

much the same way he treated his own children, who were older than we and who, more often than not, were off doing their own thing. For instance, he had a boat anchored at a sailing club on Davis Islands and he took us sailing. The first time the boat tilted all of us boys gasped in horror, worried that it was about to flip and we, who didn't know how to swim, would land in the water and drown. Once Bob asked us if we had ever gone fishing and we said: "Yeah, yeah, sure!" But our comical inexperience during our fishing expedition made clear that our yeses were more than exaggeration.

Bob belonged to a yacht club of sorts, and we would sometimes go there for meals and recreation. What was extraordinary about the place, for me at least, was that its members were diverse in a way that I had never known: Asians, African-Americans, Latinos, whites, women and men, all of a certain class and seemingly to the yacht-club born. Everything about the place felt so near yet so far away: Bob wanted us to know what might lie in store for us if we stayed out of trouble. We would talk about things that immediately concerned us, eager as we boys were for the insights of a father figure.

Sometimes Bob would drive us back home from our Saturday outings and we would caution him not to take us all the way into Central Park Village, where a white man driving a white Volvo would have been a magnet for grief at four o'clock in the afternoon. Once we told him about one of our exploits, acting like tough guys and scaring people at gunpoint. He told us that we weren't being smart and would most assuredly find ourselves in harm's way if we kept that up. "Somebody's gonna hurt you. You can't do that. That's not even kidding around. It's got downsides you can't even see." Bob tried to instill in us the core values of the YMCA: to have sincere concern for the needs and well-being of others; to tell the truth; to treat others as we would have them treat us; to do what is right.

The Saturday after the shooting, when I went to visit Bob, I was by myself for some reason and I told him nothing about what had happened. I went about things as usual. I washed his Volvo. He told me to do it again, as I had done a poor job the first time. We then went to the yacht club and wandered around. Late that afternoon he dropped me off at a safe space near Central Park Village—no drugs, no crime—a little grocery store across from the parking lot of the Tampa Fire Department. This would be my last afternoon with Bob for nearly thirty years. The whole time, I felt the weight of what I had done, the shame of my betrayal of all that Bob had tried to offer me.

THE YEAR GRANDMA LINDA LEFT FOR Georgia was also the year my mother tested positive for HIV. I found it difficult to wrap my head around her living with an infection that most assuredly would one day claim her life. It was intolerable to imagine that I was going to be motherless—and I didn't know when. I knew the man she got it from, Herbert. He used to come around and stay with Momma sometimes and play with me when he wasn't up in her room behind closed doors. Years later, she would drive me in her gray Pinto to the cemetery. We would walk to his tombstone; she would kneel and put flowers on his grave, and whisper things to him that I couldn't make out.

At Morgan Woods Elementary, I was in Mrs. Kean's third-grade class. I found it now impossible for me to sit still. I was constantly fidgeting at my desk. Unbidden, I would blurt answers out. Often, when assigned a reading or writing exercise, I would finish way ahead of everyone else. I would begin tapping, sometimes even banging, on my desk, trying to get the attention of other students, who were concentrating on completing their assignment. I would raise my hand to go to the bathroom with a suspicious frequency. Sometimes Mrs. Kean thought I was faking it, merely being a nuisance, and would ignore me. In anger, I would show her up: I would pee on myself right then and there, sitting at my desk. The piss would soak through my pants, wet my seat, and spill onto the floor. Furious, Mrs. Kean would order me to the bathroom to clean myself up as my classmates whooped and hollered. It didn't take long for me to be labeled "emotionally handicapped" and assigned to the EH class, where there were five or six other students.

. . . .

OVER THE NEXT FOUR YEARS, I WOULD attend four different public schools, where I would be routinely removed from classrooms, receive paddlings, detentions, and suspensions, and be given work far below my intellectual abilities—because of my inability to sit still. It has only been in recent years that I have learned that what I was dealing with was likely the profound dysregulation commonly seen in children living in contexts defined by chaos, violence, and abuse. The symptoms of the trauma and terror of my life at home were met with punishment, rejection, and ridicule in the school context. And by sixth grade, I was brimming with hurt, anger, and resentment. In the sixth grade I began to get into serious trouble and ultimately spent more time in facilities than in my mother's home. Prior to sixth grade, I had grown accustomed to getting picked on and beat up for my looks and manner by other kids in the neighborhood. All of that would change in 1988 and '89 when my body went through a sudden growth spurt and, for once, I was bigger and stronger than the kids who targeted me. I gained respect among the older boys and was included in their robberies and drug deals. Robert E. Lee Elementary was on Columbus Drive in the middle of Tampa Heights, a short walk from Central Park. This is where I became Jim-Jim, no longer Lil Jim-Jim. In my memories, I seemed to spend more time fighting and suspended than in the classroom.

My first arrest was in sixth grade when, during one of my suspensions, a group of older boys and I attempted a series of stick-ups that resulted in a gain of maybe five dollars. All of us were sent to W. T. Edwards Juvenile Detention Center. At age 11, this was my first time in detention and my sentence was twenty-one days—an eternity to me at the time. W. T. Edwards was on West Buffalo, the street that was later renamed Martin Luther King Boulevard. It sat in front of Hillsborough Halfway House, near Tampa Stadium. As we were being processed, a staff member said, "I hope you know how to fight, because you're going to have to get down in here."

"Even if we don't mess with nobody?"

"This is W. T. Edwards. You're going to fight whether you mess with somebody or not. Because if you don't mess with some-body, best believe somebody is going to mess with you."

THREE DAYS AFTER THE SHOOTING, I STOLE a white, four-door Cadillac Fleetwood, with two friends, ages fifteen and sixteen. We had never stolen cars to sell them; we simply wanted the feeling of being free and easy as we drove through all kinds of neighborhoods.

Now I could never figure out the mechanics of car stealing, though I had seen guys do it. All I knew was how to start the car. I had done this on a few occasions.

Soon the blare of sirens seemed to be coming from everywhere. We jumped out of the car, each running in different directions. Once out of sight, I began walking calmly to appear uninvolved. But all of a sudden a police car pulled up next to me and an officer leapt out with a K-9 barking violently (I am terrified of dogs).

"Get on the ground. Get on the ground."

He called for his partner to handcuff me, which the partner did aggressively, before leading me to the back of another squad car, which had just screeched to a stop. Now both cars gave chase to my friends. We were arrested near Hyde Park, on the west side of Tampa.

At the police station I said I was "Ian Emmanuel" because "Ian E. Manuel" was on a one-week home pass from a juvenile program. The police ran my name and it came back clean—otherwise I would not have been eligible to be released to parental custody. Obie, Ron, and I were each allowed one phone call. Ron called his mom, as did Obie. I called Momma Dump's, where my mom was often to be found.

"Is Peggye there?"

"No, Jim-Jim, she isn't here but she was here earlier."

"I'm in the police station and I need her to come get me."

"OK, Jim-Jim, if I see her I'll tell her."

I said OK and hung up. By now Obie's mom had come to fetch him. So now it was down to Ron and me.

"Ron, when your mom comes in, tell 'em we're kin so I can go with you."

"My mom won't do that, Jim-Jim."

I was allowed one more call, and I tried Momma Dump's again. Peggye was still not back.

Hours later, while sitting in one of the holding cells, I spotted the white police officer who three days earlier had thought I fit the description of the suspect in a shooting downtown.

"Excuse me, Officer, do you remember me from the other night?"

He looked at me for a second: "Yeah, why?"

"Just wanted to know if y'all caught whoever shot that lady."

"I don't think we ever did."

My conscience was gnawing at me.

OBIE, RON, AND I WERE ARRESTED AT around six o'clock, an hour and a half or so after we had stolen the Cadillac in Hyde Park. It was between nine and ten o'clock when I found myself handcuffed in the back of a squad car shooting the breeze with a police officer on our way to W. T. Edwards, twenty minutes away, where I would be held until my mom could be found.

"Boy, what you doin' stealing cars? What you doin' with those older hoodlums?"

"I grew up with those guys. We do this all the time."

The officer and I chatted about all kinds of things. I regaled him with tales of my life as a child criminal. When we reached the detention center's parking lot, he put the car in park and turned the ignition off.

"Is there anything else you wanna tell me before we get out of the car? It'll stay in the car."

"Are you for real?"

"Believe me."

"You know that lady that got shot downtown the other night? I did it."

In his deposition, the officer would claim that he then proceeded to read me my Miranda rights. He did not. What he did do was tell me that I had to remain in the car while he made a quick call in the detention center. This was not what I wanted to hear: Ten minutes or so later, the officer reappeared, turned the car on, and threw it in reverse.

"Hey, man, what you doin'?"

"I've got to take you downtown. There's a detective that wants to see you."

"Man, I don't want to go back downtown to talk to nobody. I want to go inside and sleep!"

"I'll get you back here as soon as we're finished. It won't take long. You hungry?"

"Yeah."

"I'll stop and get us something to eat on the way to the station. Relax, get some sleep until we get there."

He stopped at a Popeyes drive-thru for chicken and biscuits; I could no longer keep my eyes open and fell asleep in the back of the squad car until arriving back at the police station. When we got back downtown, we walked through the back of the station, where I was introduced to the detective: he was standing in front of a table with stacks of hundred-dollar bills, presumably in the wake of a drug bust. The detective and officer led me upstairs. The officer took my handcuffs off, gave me the box of chicken and biscuits and a soda, and asked me to sign a waiver of some kind. After the detective read me my Miranda rights, I reconstructed the shooting for him—he had said that the faster I told him what happened, the sooner I would be able to get some rest. The interrogation over, I was driven back to W. T. Edwards. The next day, I was taken to juvenile court and sentenced to twenty-one days for grand theft auto.

A COUPLE OF WEEKS WENT BY AND I STILL wasn't charged with the shooting. I frequently stopped by the open classification window in W. T. Edwards and asked Ms. Matthews to check if I had any pending charges or holds. She would look through paperwork and at her database and reply, "Nope, you're fine. You should be out soon." I didn't know what was going on. I was fearful police were waiting until the very end of my twenty-one-day sentence to charge me so that I would have to serve an additional twenty-one days.

Around my eighteenth day in W. T., I asked the supervisor, a middle-aged brown-skinned man who wore thick glasses, to assign me to clean the hallway. Sweeping the long expanse with a wide broom allowed freedom of movement from dorm to dorm. Soon a staff member approached me.

"Manuel, the supervisor want you. He around there waiting in front of classification."

I hurried around the corner and saw him talking to a black detective wearing a sharp suit.

"Manuel, I'm forgetting your brother's name. What's it again?"

"Sean Manuel, but they call him John-John."

The supervisor said to the detective, "Yeah, that's it, Sean Manuel—you remember him?"

"Oh, yeah, I remember that boy."

I said, "I'll go get the broom and start sweeping."

"No you ain't. You going to jail. Detective Dessau is here to arrest your ass."

"Man, stop playing. What you got me out here for?"

"Nigga, I ain't playing. I'm as serious as cancer. You going to the county jail. You done made it to the big time now."

FOR DAYS AFTER I SHOT HER, DEBBIE BAIGRIE sat at her front window, terrified and fearful that I might show up to finish her off. A petite, pretty blonde, Debbie, then twenty-eight, was mother to two daughters, a toddler and an infant. Debbie had grown up in a nice Tampa neighborhood, the scion of a family with Orthodox Jewish roots. She was now married to an electrical engineer and had been living a relatively comfortable life.

On the sweltering evening of July 27, 1990, Debbie met up with two girlfriends in downtown Tampa for a rare dinner out—her first such night after the birth of her one-year-old. As she left the restaurant to go to her parked car, she ran into a fellow gym member; he advised her that the neighborhood was unsafe and offered to accompany her to the parking lot. It was then that calamity struck, causing her to wonder what kind of face she still had. As she would later tell a reporter:[1] "The sound of that gun was louder than I could have ever imagined. A bullet entered my open mouth, tore through my teeth and went out through my cheek. Staggering back into the restaurant, blood streaming from my face, I screamed, 'Help me! I've been shot!' I was too panic-stricken to be conscious of any pain; the only thing I felt was fear.

"My wound was not life threatening. But five teeth had been shot out, a portion of my gums was destroyed and there was a small bullet hole in my cheek." So began Debbie's decades-long ordeal—more than forty oral surgery interventions—to reconstruct her mouth. When days later she found out that she had been shot by a thirteen-year-old, she was incredulous: "Why, he's just a child!" she exclaimed. At thirteen years of age, I was charged as an adult with multiple offenses: robbery, attempted robbery, and two counts of attempted murder in the first degree. Florida law allowed for a child of any age to be tried as an adult if indicted for a life-or-death felony. As I would later learn, no allowance was necessary. Because of my juvenile record and the gravity of the charges I now faced, state law mandated that I be sentenced as if I were an adult. Assistant State Attorney Hank Lavandera put it this way: "As it now appears, based on his prior record, he could face a life sentence if convicted of these charges."[2]

THE MORNING OF MY SENTENCING HEAR-ing I woke up in Morgan Street County Jail, to which I had been remanded on August 17; it sat right across from my old neighborhood. I had spent most of my confinement on the juvenile floor (juveniles, ages thirteen to seventeen, were housed away from adults). We were on the third floor, where they used to incarcerate women, whom they had moved to a newly constructed facility—Orient Road Jail. On the juvenile floor there were six cells numbered from 3A1 to 3A6. I spent most of my time in 3A2; it was packed with kids from Central Park Village, there for robbery, grand theft auto, drug possession, and trafficking. Each cell had eight bunk beds, though each more often than not housed twelve to sixteen inmates. This meant that now and then some of us had to sleep on mattresses placed on tables in the TV room and on its floor.

Our cellblock was riddled with fighting and cruel juvenile mayhem. Kids asleep might wake up wrapped in toilet paper and on fire (the contraband matches having been secured from an adult inmate). Or toilet paper would be rolled into tight wicks, which were jabbed into their nostrils or between their toes and lit.

I had seniority, after my numerous stints in juvenile detention centers, and a reputation for backing down from no one. I got respect for my fighting skills. Now and then I would look out for kids who were slated for rough times. I'd sneak up and tell them, "Listen, they going to try to jump you after chow. You need to ask for a cell change." Some listened and saved themselves. Some didn't and left on stretchers. I took a liking to one white kid in particular—William Bartfield, and did not allow anybody to mess with him. William told his mom I was looking out for him and she began putting money into my account. I was surprised and grateful for the gesture, but I naturally gravitated toward those I considered underdogs like myself.

All the same, seniority and fighting skills aside, I still pissed on myself while sleeping. This didn't stop until my fourteenth birthday, two weeks before my sentencing. It just stopped abruptly.

SINCE AROUND THE END OF JANUARY, I HAD been in solitary confinement. I had flung, through the bars into the wing, a cup of water with which I was supposed to have gulped down some kind of medication (it may have been a painkiller; the drugs administered to me were not yet psychotropic). At first, the guards didn't know who was responsible for the vandalism, but when they threatened confiscation of the cell's TV, I had no choice but to confess, resulting in a fiery dispute with the deputy and a nurse.

The cell I inhabited was minuscule. If I had to estimate its dimensions, I would say that at its widest I could take no more than five steps in the size eight shoes that I wore at the time. There was a narrow bunk bed near the window; I fit it comfortably as I was only five foot seven. That window became a source of fascination to me. Soon after I found myself in solitary, the Super Bowl took place in Tampa, and believe it or not that night I could see the lights of Tampa Stadium from my cell. They shone exceedingly bright. I imagined the rampant excitement of people from all walks of life in the stadium and watching the game on TV all over the world. I later learned that Whitney Houston had sung the national anthem, this during the Desert Storm war. I stared at the window and was overwhelmed by a longing for home; I don't know if you can realize how it feels to be so close to home, yet so very far away. I was gripped by sadness and cheered myself by imagining attending a future Super Bowl.

LATE FEBRUARY I HAD AN APPOINTMENT with my court-assigned attorney downtown for a motion to suppress my confession, which was the only hard evidence connecting me to the crime. A deputy escorted me into the cold courtroom and led me to the jury box, where juveniles usually sat away from adult prisoners. I found a seat among the sparse crowd of spectators. My lawyer, Brian Gonzalez, hobbled over to me (still on crutches from a torn Achilles tendon, I believe) and said, "Hey, Ian, how are you doing this morning?"

"I'm good. Just ready to go to trial so I can go home."

It was February 22, 1991, and I had been arrested on July 30, 1990. Nearly seven months had passed; I had never been locked down for this long.

"Yeah, that's what I want to talk to you about."

"What's up?"

"I need you to consider changing your plea to an open plea of guilt."

"What's that?"

"It's a plea where you throw yourself at the mercy of the court and let the judge decide what your sentence should be. Not the state. I've already talked to the judge and he has assured me that you won't get more than fifteen years."

"Fifteen years!" I said. Was this dude crazy?

I didn't want to go to prison period, let alone for fifteen years.

"Yeah, I know it sounds like a long time, but it's better than life. And I'm going to argue for a youthful offender sentence, which is far less than that. All you have to do is plead guilty."

"I don't want to go to prison. Can't you try to get me life probation or something like that?"

"Ian, you're going to have to do some time, but if you go to trial, you'll make the judge mad and he'll give you life for sure. So what's it going to be?"

I shook my head no; I wasn't pleading guilty.

While my lawyer and I went back and forth, my mom had been sitting among other spectators, watching us. My lawyer hobbled over and sat down beside her. They whispered to each other intensely.

After about five minutes, my lawyer escorted my mom over to the side of the jury box.

She said, "Baby, do what your lawyer say and plead guilty so you'll get a chance to come home. I don't want you to get life. That would break my heart."

"Ma, I don't wanna go to prison, period."

"Please, Jim, do it for me. Do this one thing for me. Don't think about yourself just this one time."

At that moment it seemed to me that every time I had gone against my momma's wishes and done things my way, I had come up short. I looked with my tear-filled eyes at hers and said, "All right, Ma."

ON THE MORNING OF APRIL 11—AT AROUND 5:30; it was before dawn—juveniles at Morgan Street County Jail who were to be sentenced or who had court appointments were herded, handcuffed, into a van that would take us to the courthouse downtown. Anxious as I was about what would happen, I was certain about two things: the worst-case scenario, which to my teenage mind was no different from a life imprisonment, would be the fifteen-year sentence that my attorney had promised—with good behavior I would serve no more than ten; the best-case scenario would be my fantasy of life probation, which I had asked my attorney to request. I had heard too many horror stories about life in prison from grownups to want to spend even a single day there. At the courthouse, we were ushered into holding cells corresponding to our respective judges. Mine was the Honorable Manuel Menendez, Jr., renowned for his severity. In my holding cell was a guy I used to call "cousin," though we were unrelated. We grew up in Central Park Village; my mom and his, whom I called Aunt Louise, were very good friends. When I had gotten out of juvenile detention the previous year, I had stayed at his house. His name was Sam. He was facing a petty trespassing charge. When they came to get me for sentencing, hours after I had arrived, he said, "Good luck, I'm praying for you"—or some such thing.

It was before 8:30 a.m. when I was led into the courtroom and assigned to the jury box with another juvenile to await the beginning of the hearing. In the audience were my mother; Betty Walker, my maternal grandmother; Bob Gilbertson; Debbie Baigrie; and the man who had walked Debbie to her car that night. "I went to the courthouse to see him sentenced," Debbie would later recall.[3] "After my initial fear had passed, I'd become plain angry. But when I saw him in court, my rage seemed to leave me. He looked so young and alone, among all the attorneys and law-enforcement officers who were there." The State of Florida was represented by Karen Cox, and I, the defendant, by Brian Gonzalez. My public defender began the proceedings by re-citing the difficult circumstances of my back-ground and upbringing—emphasizing that I had never had a strong male role model—not to excuse my run-ins with the law, my criminal history, but to explain my actions as perhaps caused by my environment and warranting leniency. "No one can argue,"[4] he said, "with the seriousness of these offenses. It's a horrifying situation that we stand before the court and we're not here to make excuses. There is no doubt Ian Manuel has failed at his attempt regarding juvenile sanctions."

Karen Cox, the assistant state attorney, agreed that I had a terrible background and had been unresponsive to juvenile sanctions. Rather than leniency, however, she called on the judge to dispose of me. At thirteen, I was a problem with no solution. Cox concluded: "It may be a comment on our society that we can have a thirteen-year-old who comes to us with this type of background and no prospect of rehabilitation . . . There is no solution to this problem and the only thing we can do is protect the citizens from the future criminal conduct that Mr. Manuel will engage in if he is released. I would ask that he be sentenced to life in prison as the sentencing guidelines call for."

Cox was advancing a prevalent view at the time about boys of color, a view that would achieve enduring notoriety with Hillary Clinton's infamous 1996 remarks at the apex of anxiety about high rates of crime and violence during her husband's administration: **"They are often the kinds of kids that are called super predators. No conscience. No empathy. We can talk about why they ended up that way but first we have to bring them to heel."**[5]

Cox then inquired whether Debbie Baigrie wanted to address the court. Debbie said, "No, not right now."[6]

The court invited my mother to speak. She said, "I really don't know what to say. I have done the best I can for Ian and I don't believe there is nothing that can't be done. Something has to be done for my child. Like the lawyer, I agree it's the environment. These people take these things for every day occurrences. They feel like this is what people do.

"I tried to tell him this isn't the way. Maybe now it will sink in. There is another side to life. The first time he was arrested, I was at HCC [a community college] in a juvenile course trying to see what's wrong with my children because both of them had gone astray. I don't know.

"Something has to be done, not be locked away for the rest of his life. I don't feel that's the answer. He can't get away with it, because that wouldn't be the right answer either. If someone shot me, they would be ready to call them up. I feel like—I don't know. I don't want him locked away for the rest of his life, but he has to be punished."

My public defender prefaced his presentation of Bob Gilbertson as a character witness by saying: "Judge, there is another side to Ian Manuel. Unfortunately, what the court has heard so far, it would indicate that he's a human being with not one ounce of good within his body."

Bob, whose support of me was undying, and who had been sending me a few dollars now and then while I was in the county jail, recalled my dealings with him:

"During this time, there was never really any—I understood there were things going on with Ian. I wasn't privy to exactly what was happening with regard to other criminal activity, but all of the time that he spent with us and at the Y, he acted just like any of the other kids that we have.

"His interaction with other kids on field trips, of which he took a number, was always excellent and there were never any problems with other kids, never any problems with authorities relative to complying with what he was asked to do.

"I would draw from that to some extent that if Ian were kept active and were at the point—kept supervised, he knows how to behave and he knows how to do the right things. It's the less supervised kind of setting it appears he has difficulty in . . . We work with a lot of kids all the time from a lot of different environments and it would be our hope that there could be something done where he could continue to get some education and some trade so that if he is released, he would have something he could do with his life from that point on."

Brian Gonzalez then pleaded to the judge for leniency:

"If Mr. Ian Manuel is sentenced as the State or the PSI would suggest, I believe we would be disregarding his last chance although it would be his first chance as an adult at the age of fourteen to allow him to function among us, among you and I and everyone else that exists in this community.

"Apparently, it's become quite obvious to all of us that he cannot function right now. We are resolved in that matter and we don't attempt to sit here and tell the court he should not be going to Florida State Prison. I believe his crimes suggest he should go to Florida State Prison. It is obvious he does have good within him. There is no doubt in my mind in my interaction with him that there is something there. It's obvious his values have not been molded properly. It's too young for him to be etched in stone, to be disregarded to a life or substantial amount of years in prison."

Something then happened that has haunted me ever since. The juvenile prisoner sitting next to me in the jury box said something funny, and I laughed. Debbie saw this and it understandably angered her. She felt that I did not understand the gravity of my actions and the impact they had and continued to have on her. She was right. I did not understand. I was fourteen years old and I just wanted to go home. It would take years for me to understand.

Debbie decided to address the court:

"Your Honor, I was listening to the Public Defender talking about how Mr. Manuel didn't have a father as a role model. Neither did I. It didn't make me go out and shoot people. They said the gun went off by accident. It was aimed in my face. I don't think it went off by accident.

"From the time this started, I should have been angry. I should have been angry at him and angry at his parents. I wasn't angry. I felt like he was as victimized as I was because of where he came from. He was a product of his own environment and he is as much of a victim as I am.

"I kept speaking to everybody, please rehabilitate him. He's young. I have two children. I know it takes work constant every day— every day I do something with my children. I think this is going to affect them for the rest of their lives. He's still a child.

"Until yesterday, I kept thinking, I wish he could be rehabilitated. I wish that he could be made an example of. If he could go from doing this to making something of himself, getting an education and doing something with his life instead of spending the rest of his life in prison, it hurts me to think that somebody should have to do that at such a young age and have no chance of a life.

"But after hearing everything that's been going on, he doesn't even care. He doesn't care what he's done to me. He doesn't care that he's going to spend the rest of his life in jail. And if he doesn't care, well, I don't care."

There was a hush in the courtroom. I have no way of knowing whether Judge Menendez was at all swayed by Debbie's remarks. He seemed already to have made up his mind when he took command and pronounced his stern judgment:

"The prospects for adequate protection of the public and likelihood for reasonable rehabilitation of the child if assigned to juvenile services and facilities considering all these factors, I find would be none, absolutely no chance of that happening for juvenile sanctions . . .

"I do find at this time and determine that adult sanctions are suitable and should in fact be imposed against the Defendant in this particular case.

"With regard to each of these offenses at this time, it is the judgment, order and sentence of the Court, first of all, that you be adjudicated guilty of each of these offenses of robbery, attempted robbery and two counts of attempted murder in the first degree . . .

"Your attorney has indicated and asks the Court to consider imposing sentence because of the fact of your age and your environment.

"I think that in one sense, while your environment may have played a part in the situation you're finding yourself in, I cannot for the life of me understand how anyone could actually say the environment is the cause of your conduct.

"If that was the case, there are a number of other people that live in your environment, your mother, for example, and she's not going out there and committing the atrocious acts that you've committed.

"Our society, I think, does require incarceration for some period of time, a substantial period of time, if for no other reason than to protect itself from you. A comment was made here that perhaps would provide for one last chance, one opportunity to allow you to prove that you can become a productive member of society.

"As you might have noted here, you've been given a number of chances. After a while, you run out of chances. There are some acts whether you've been given prior chances or not, there just is no second chance available. I think you've crossed that line."[7]

For count one, robbery, Judge Menendez sentenced me at age fourteen to life in prison without parole. For count two, attempted robbery, he sentenced me to fifteen years incarceration to run concurrently. For count three, the attempted murder of Debbie in the first degree, he sentenced me to life without parole. For count four, the attempted murder of the man who walked Debbie to her car, Judge Menendez sentenced me to life probation on top of my life without parole sentences, "in the event the Department of Corrections for some reason should release you from incarceration."

I was struck by my helplessness in the light of his omnipotence. In retrospect, I feel that I was being tried not only for the crimes that I had committed but for proof that I had a right to exist.

When you are a kid being sentenced, your mom can stand with you. When my mom heard the judge's declaration, she understood the enormity of his intention. She hugged me tight. She was crying. My face pressed against her, I refused to cry, not in front of strangers. My own tears would come later. As the bailiff gently, but firmly, pulled me away from my mom toward the fingerprint area, little did I know that that would be the last time my mother and I would touch.

. . .

AS I WAS LED BACK TO THE HOLDING CELL,
I was robotic, a chaos of feelings churning
inside of me—anger at the judge, terror at
not knowing what lay ahead, fear of what
could happen to me in prison. Not used to—
perhaps incapable of—showing vulnerability
to strangers, or anyone else for that matter (a
danger where I came from), I numbed myself
to the overwhelming hurt I felt.

When I walked into the holding cell Sam
said: "Man, what did they do, Jim? What
did they do?" For some reason in my mind,
I don't know why, each life sentence didn't
mean my whole life, didn't mean I would die
in prison; each meant twenty years, already
an eternity to me. So I told Sam they gave me
forty years.

"What? Stop lying. You always playing,
man. What did they give you?"

"They gave me forty years."

"What? You for real?"

"Yeah, man."

Sam was the only inmate left in the holding
cell, and I was glad he was there. I needed a
familiar face, someone around whom I could

be myself. He repeated, "You for real, Jim?" and he just started crying. He kept pounding his fist into his hand and saying, "I'm gon' kill all them crackers when I get out." His tears gave me permission to release my pent-up emotions. I cried as well; we hugged. I was surprised: I had never seen Sam cry except when his mom whipped him. Now both of us were sobbing in the holding cell before we were handcuffed together and returned by van to the county jail. Most days, I still think about that moment with Sam, the way my sentence, and the hopelessness of it hurt him too. What does it mean for one child to see another sent—deliberately, methodically, and under the moral authority of the adults in charge—into the heart of darkness?

OCEAN SHELL

I press my ear canal—
against the interior of my ocean shell.
Just longing to hear the water.
But my attempts all fail.
And what comes through my ears—
are echoes of the hopeless.
I hear coughs & gaggings
from multiple gassings.
And boots & fist against flesh.
Sounds of desperation.
From victims of devastation.
Releasing another exasperated breath.
I hear the sound of shivers—
from prisoners in the cold of winter
with nothing to cover their bodies.
I hear the cardboard fan—
in the prisoner's hand.
To combat the sweltering summer.
I hear the groans & mumblings.
And the goings & comings—
of past occupants who remain
    anonymous.
I hear the ultimate suffering.

Hunger reminiscent of thunder
An orchestra of grumbling stomachs.
I hear noises & voices.
From unknown sources.
And the unmistakable sound
     of crying.
I hear prisoners taunted.
and tormentors confronted.
By those with nothing to lose but
     their minds.
But where is the water?
The wonderful ocean—
I originally longed to hear.
With this cell by my ear.
The only water I hear—
is the repeated patter of tears.

. . .

WHEN I AM LED TO THE THIRD FLOOR (I've been ordered out of solitary confinement), cell 3A2 is packed with my homeboys from Central Park, one of whom is Marquis, who had participated in my crime but was never arrested for it. He was in the county jail for another robbery.

"Jim-Jim, what'd they do, what'd they do?"

"Nothin' but life, nothin' but life," I said, chuckling, recovering bravado. I refused to show the pain I was in. I was implying as loudly as possible "I can handle this." Marquis and I, of course, had grown up together, and he regarded me as someone with a lot of heart, a lot of courage; I didn't want to show him my fear. By law, after my sentencing, I was no longer a juvenile but an adult and would soon be put among the adult men on the first floor. I had only a few hours to prepare for the transition, and I tried to visualize how I would defend myself against what might face me there. Adult inmates sharing cells, after all, were renowned for viciously beating each other up. Stretchers were always being carried in and out of those cells. I hoped to be placed among older homeboys who might know, and look out for, me.

When the officer came to fetch me, he announced that I would be transferred to Orient Road Jail. He was leading me to a holding cell where, by myself, I would wait for the van that would take me to my new prison. The officer and I took the elevator down, I, dressed in a light blue jumpsuit and toting my sheets, cup for drinking water, toothbrush and toothpaste, and, inside my pillowcase, letters my mom had written me. As I walked slowly toward the holding cell before heading to Orient Road Jail, a sergeant barked: "Uh-uh, don't be walking all slow now. You goin' with the big boys. You wanted to be a big boy? You a big boy now. They got somethin' for you over there."

At Orient Road Jail, I didn't have to be processed; I was already in the system. I was shocked. The first floor of Orient Road seemed like the biggest hotel lobby in the world, wide enough to fit two tractor-trailers side by side and as long as a football field—or so it seemed to me. Men and women inmates commingled there, sitting around chatting. I was led down the hallway to 6 Charlie; I had no idea what 6 Charlie was, but it turned out to be solitary confinement. I was uncuffed and put alone into a single cell. It was brand-new, the paint was so fresh you could smell it. It was cold in there. They kept it cold in there. That was OK. What disturbed me was that everything was purple. The door was purple. The walls were purple. The rails were purple. The concrete slab that you put your mattress on was purple. Perplexed, I asked the first officer making his rounds: "Sir, please can you tell me why I'm in confinement and why everything is purple?" I learned from him that I was in solitary because of my age, fourteen, and because of the length of my sentence, life imprisonment. As to why everything was purple, psychologists had decided that the color had a calming effect on inmates.

It was now around 9:30 p.m., twelve hours or so after I had been sentenced. I was numb, interred in all that purple—in solitary confinement as I had been when I woke up, but with a life sentence now hanging over me. I dwelled on the events of the day: I thought about my impulsive laughter in the courtroom, wondering if that was what sealed my fate; about Debbie's heartfelt remarks; about my mom, who was HIV positive, and whether she would be alive when I got out. I held on to a glimmer of hope. My lawyer had said at sentencing: "Don't worry, we're going to appeal; don't worry, we're going to appeal."

I fell asleep from exhaustion.

ABOUT TWO WEEKS AFTER I WAS SEN-tenced, I was taken by surprise and hurried back to court. I thought the appeal my lawyer had mentioned was at hand. Before the hearing, I asked him: "What am I doing here? Is this the appeal you told me about?"

"No, no, Ian, that'll come later. You're here because the judge forgot to give you three years mandatory. The law in Florida says that because you carried a firearm you have to be sentenced to a mandatory minimum of three years. The judge doesn't have a choice in this, so since he forgot, I let him know. I brought it to his attention so it'll look good on your appeal."

I now found myself standing before the man who had already condemned me to die in prison, waiting for him to give me more time.

4

"HEY, BOY, WHAT'S YOUR NAME?" A FAT WHITE correctional officer seated behind a desk at the Reception and Medical Center asked me.

"Ian Manuel."

"How old is you, boy?"

"Fourteen, sir."

"Fourteen. One of y'all call K Wing and tell 'em we got another one of them pop-eyed ass jitterbugs for 'em. Sign this paper here and stand down there at the end of the line away from the grownups."

The Reception and Medical Center is a state prison in Lake Butler, Florida—a part of Union County—about one and one-half hours from Tampa (I would not see Tampa again for nine years). On May 11 I had been transferred to Lake Butler. Offenders are taken there not only for medical treatment but for initial classification and processing into the state correctional system. Lake Butler was well known as an exceptionally brutal place. Even as young boys in Central Park, we had heard tales from returning ex-cons about its viciousness: how the guards hated blacks from Miami and inmates who wore red Converse sneakers; how they had a jar filled with gold teeth that they had kicked out of inmates' mouths. Some of these gold teeth had supposedly been implanted into the mouths of K-9s. And if you got caught committing a minor infraction in open population, sometimes the guards would make you sweep the sun off the sidewalk, that is, push a broom across an already spotless sidewalk until sundown. "Driving a Cadillac" meant walking around the sprawling Lake Butler compound with a butt can, picking up cigarette butts all day long as punishment. Widely notorious guards, like "Nigger Johnson," and K Wing Freddie, were said to have beaten and killed many an inmate over the years in the cellblock known as K Wing—the confinement wing of Lake Butler. Because of my age, I was assigned to K Wing, where adolescents were segregated, to begin the rest of my life in prison.

"THE LAW TREATS ADOLESCENTS DIFFER-ently because they are different," says the Equal Justice Initiative's landmark report **Cruel and Unusual: Sentencing 13- and 14-Year-Old Children to Die in Prison.**[1] "Using state-of-the-art imaging technology, scientists have revealed that adolescents' brains are anatomically undeveloped in parts of the cerebrum associated with impulse control, regulation of emotions, risk assessment, and moral reasoning. Accordingly, the neurological development most critical to making good judgments, moral and ethical decision-making, and controlling impulsive behavior is incomplete during adolescence." The study, published in 2007, identified seventy-three children in the United States sentenced to life imprisonment without the possibility of parole for crimes committed when they were thirteen or fourteen years old. Of those sentenced for nonhomicide crimes, I was one. Among the report's key findings are these:

The United States is the only country in the world known to have condemned thirteen- and fourteen-year-old children to imprisonment until death.

Most of these children were accomplices to adults or older teens who were more culpable for the crime.

Seven, or roughly 10 percent, of the seventy-three children were convicted of crimes in which no one was killed. In one case, no one was even injured. All seven are children of color.

Six states have condemned thirteen-year-old children to imprisonment until death. All but one of these children are racial minorities.

Most of the seventy-three children suffered years of severe abuse and neglect. Some tried to commit suicide as young as age eight.

Judges in the vast majority of these cases were forced to impose mandatory death-in-prison sentences without considering the child's age or background or the circumstances of the crime.

Children of color are disproportionately sentenced to die in prison. Of the seventy-three children identified, roughly two-thirds are people of color; nearly half are African-American.

Most of these kids are from poor families and received grossly inadequate legal representation. Court-appointed attorneys failed to file postconviction appeals and never challenged the death-in-prison sentences in most of these cases.

All of the seventy-three children have been sent to adult prisons, where many are targets of horrendous physical and sexual assault by adult inmates. One Equal Justice Initiative client attempted suicide three times after being repeatedly raped by adult inmates.

I WALKED THE LINE TO THE END OF A long brown bench by an open gate. Grown men, my fellow passengers on the sheriff's bus to Lake Butler, stood side by side along the bench. At the end of the line, several feet away from the last adult, I found my place. Corrections officers ordered us, the men and me, to strip and to open our mouths wide and run our fingers inside in a circular motion as they walked up and down the line, peering into our mouths for contraband.

They commanded us to pull our ears back and to run our fingers through our hair, then to turn around and wiggle our toes, one bare foot at a time. Finally, they forced us to bend over at the waist, pull the cheeks of our buttocks apart, and cough loudly three times. The cacophony of coughs was at once horrific and disgusting. They handed us prison garb—mine way oversized for my adolescent frame—and ushered us through a gate to some more benches, where we waited to be called to the property counter before going to see the nurse for the first time.

You have so many days to get your vaccinations and shots for diseases like tetanus. They draw blood to make sure you're not carrying diseases. They perform psychological evaluations. Dental exams. They process you supposedly to ensure placement in the most appropriate adult prison. If you have serious medical issues they'll put you in one that can offer the needed treatment, or so they say. If you have severe mental illness, they'll put you in one that can provide mental health care. (Twenty-five percent of all prisoners suffer from a mental illness, the most common being clinical depression, bipolar disorder, schizophrenia, and psychotic breaks.) You are at Butler for your overseers to develop a profile of you; theirs is an ongoing process of collecting and assessing information to determine the level of risk you might pose, the kind of confinement right for you, and other prison-related matters.

To get to K Wing a guard escorted me through the first-floor door and instructed me to jog up two flights of stairs to another door, which led to an administrative station. There was a board with slots for different-colored slips of paper. This was the housing board, and the color of a slip indicated an inmate's status: red for youthful offenders, yellow for those being disciplined; white for troublemakers causing administrative conflict, and so on. The point was to prevent officers from mixing colors, that is, housing inmates of different statuses in the same cell.

I was led to K Wing's shower, down some steps, and off to the left. I was locked in the shower for about thirty minutes before a short, fat, white corrections officer arrived. "Strip," he demanded. I said, "They already searched me." He said, "Boy, don't mother-fucking back-talk me. Just do as you're told."

I went through the motions: I took my clothes off, opened my mouth wide and circled my fingers in it, pulled my ears back. But this time the rest of the examination would be different. The guard pulled latex gloves out of his pocket and made a show of slowly putting them on and stretching the latex up to his wrists, snapping them loudly against his skin. Then he said, "All right, boy, turn around and bend over and open your ass up, and I mean real wide, and keep 'em spread until I tell you to turn around. If you don't open up wide enough for me to see if you got anything up in there, I'm going to stick my hand up there and see for myself."

Overcome with anxiety, I recalled my brother's molestation of me as a child, yet I complied with the officer's sick command. After having been bent over as the guard inspected me for about a minute, I was finally allowed to stand up straight. The guard ordered me to dress and led me to my cell.

·   ·   ·

K WING CONSISTED OF TWO TIERS OF ABOUT forty cells, twenty on the first floor and twenty in the basement. There were two steel bunks in each cell, except for the last two cells downstairs, which had none. These two cells were called "the hole," where inmates deemed unruly were sent to be broken into submissiveness. The hole was a cell with bars and an outer door that could be shut to close off all sight and sound outside.

I was placed on the second floor, in cell 4. During the twenty-three days I spent at Lake Butler, two fellow juvenile cellmates came and went; one was fourteen like me, the other older, seventeen years old, I believe. We were locked down on K Wing twenty-four hours a day; if we had to leave the building for any reason we were chained and shackled and escorted by an officer. My cellmates and I slept, ate, and did our business in a cramped four-by-eight cell with a stainless steel latrine.

We all woke up early because early morning was when transfers were announced, Mondays through Fridays. Everyone would get up hoping his name was on the list to leave that dangerous place. Back then they were killing people in Lake Butler. In confinement. They were beating people. I heard tales of gassing, though I myself didn't witness any actual instances.

At first my main preoccupation was to do nothing that might antagonize guards so I wouldn't be beaten. They, especially Officer Wilson—a slim black guy—used to slap us. If he caught you falling asleep against the wall late at night before count time was clear, he would become enraged. He'd sneak down the catwalk, trying to catch you nodding off. If you were unfortunate enough to be sleepy, he'd make you come over to him so that he could reach through the bars and slap you five or six times.

I grew severely anxious at always being at the mercy of Officer Wilson, at the prospect of being assaulted by him on the one hand and on the other because I was always hoping that when I heard them rolling the doors and telling people to pack it up I would hear "Hey, Manuel, roll it up," which meant I would be on my way out of Lake Butler. As I was having trouble falling asleep and staying asleep at night, a psychiatrist put me on Vistaril, a sedative to relieve anxiety and tension—even now, I recall the foul taste of the oral syrup. What I didn't know at the time was that taking this psychotropic medication, prescribed chiefly to induce sleep, was raising my psychiatric grade and so the risk to myself and others that prison authorities imagined I posed.

Because we hadn't committed any serious disciplinary infractions, we were allowed to order from the canteen weekly, and my mom was sending me money at the time. Of course, we bought food and snacks, but a loophole in the ordering system allowed adolescents to buy tobacco products—here in confinement we were getting away with something that would have been impossible in open population. I didn't smoke, but in prison, tobacco is big commerce. I'd order Tampa Jewels cigars and packs of Bugler tobacco. And then I'd trade my haul for extra sweets—cookies and honey buns. We traded with adults farther down the wing. Upstairs only the first six cells were for juveniles. Tobacco was so valuable that you could double your money with it. When the officer wasn't on the wing, you'd get on the bars and shout, "I got a pack of cigarettes for four packs of cookies, who call that?" Someone would say, "Hey, I call that." An adult could roll at least thirty-six cigarettes from a single pack of tobacco, so to him, trading four packs of cookies for three dozen cigarettes was a great deal. I loved peanut butter cookies then, especially when I could wash them down with a carton of Yoo-Hoo. By the way, the food at Lake Butler was good. We ate breakfast at around six, lunch at twelve, and dinner at five. Big old biscuits, scrambled eggs, bony fish—considered a delicacy by some—and slop, noodles drowned in unrecognizable sauce.

AT LAKE BUTLER I READ THE BIBLE IN-tensively to while away the hours. When I was a little boy, Grandma Linda used to take me to New Salem Baptist Church, and it was there that I first became acquainted with the book through Sunday school. Now a certain Mr. Norman—aware of the notoriety of my case—visited the prison. A Seventh-Day Adventist, he took a liking to me and ended up giving me this big black Bible. He taught me that the Book of Proverbs has thirty-one chapters, so if I read one a day, I would complete it in a month. I read around in the Bible and felt the tug of religion, felt the comfort it offered. One of my favorite passages is from Proverbs 30:

> **Four things on earth are small,**
> **yet they are extremely wise:**
> **Ants are creatures of little strength,**
> **yet they store up their food in**
> **the summer;**
> **hyraxes are creatures of little power,**
> **yet they make their home in the crags;**
> **locusts have no king,**
> **yet they advance together in ranks;**
> **a lizard can be caught with the hand,**
> **yet it is found in kings' palaces.**[2]

Regardless of my hazy understanding of what I read, these passages seemed vaguely to speak to my condition, and for this I cherished them. Looking back now, I think this was where my interest in poetry may have begun. These words and images and the comfort and strength they gave me was powerful in a way

I don't understand—but they planted a seed of hope in me that I would find my way out, back to my mother, back to my home, and—most dangerously—that I was somebody.

ONE SATURDAY, I HEARD AN OFFICER YELL "Clean up," as a cellblock trusty walked down the tier sticking brooms through the bars. When he got to my cell, I told him I didn't want the broom. The officer said, "You got to clean up." I said, "Sir, today is the Sabbath and it's against my religion to do any work on this day." He said, "Boy, is you crazy? Today is Saturday. The day of rest is Sunday. And what you talkin' about? Inmates work seven days a week up in here. Sweep the fucking cell." I refused. He went and got the sarge, who took his turn ordering me to sweep the cell. Again I refused. I felt this was what Jesus wanted me to do. Stand up for him despite the consequences. I explained my reasons to the sarge. The sarge left. About thirty minutes later, the officer returned to my cell with handcuffs and said, "The captain wants to talk to you." My hands were cuffed behind my back and I was escorted down the steps of the tier onto the quarterback deck and into the sergeant's station. The door closed behind me. The sarge was seated at the desk, and I was ordered to stand in front of the black captain who was also in the office. I read his name tag. It said "Jones." I was standing before the notorious officer everyone referred to as "Nigger Johnson."

The sergeant said: "Boy, tell the captain what you told me."

"Sir, Sunday is the first day of the week, Saturday is the last. Today is the Sabbath day and it's against my religion to sweep my cell today."

Without hesitation, Captain Jones swung a heavy-handed slap my way. I ducked. Captain Jones then swung again with his left hand; again I evaded his attempt. As I bobbed and weaved, my hands cuffed behind my back, I made a calculation I would need to make repeatedly over the coming years as I learned to navigate the labyrinth of Florida DOC power games. I realized that if I kept embarrassing "Nigger Johnson" in front of his staff he would make a point of hurting me as bad as he could. When the captain swung again,

I stood my ground. He slapped me hard on the left and right sides of my face four or five times. I said nothing. I just stood there, crying silently.

"Boy, where you from?"

"Tampa."

"How old you is?"

"Fourteen."

"Fourteen!"

"Yeah, and I'm a get my momma to call HRS on you." (That is the Florida Department of Health and Rehabilitative Services.)

"Boy, I don't care nothing about no HRS. Is you gon' clean that cell now?"

"No sir," I said.

"If you don't clean up, boy, I'm a put you in the hole. And when I put little motherfuckers like you in the hole, I likes to beat 'em while they choking on the gas I done sprayed on them. So what you gon' do?"

"I'm not cleaning my cell on the Sabbath, sir."

"Put his ass in the hole."

An officer led me out of the sergeant's station, down the steps of the first-floor tier, past the shower, and down the long hallway to the second to last cell on K Wing. I walked through the outer door and then the cell bar door, which the officer manually closed. He uncuffed me, then walked out, closing the outer door behind him. I sat down on the bare mattress, wondering if I had done the right thing and waiting for a beating and gassing that never came. That night, I woke up to huge cockroaches crawling over my body. I jumped out of my sleep and brushed them off my torso onto the floor of the dark cell. I couldn't go back to sleep because I didn't know if rats would show up next. What showed up next, though, was a white corrections officer with what looked like a permanent crook in his neck. Entering my cell, he began slapping and punching me in my face and on my head for two to three minutes. Cowering, I tried to cover my head with my arms. He exited the cell as quickly as he had entered it, closing the outer door behind him.

In my rage and fear, I got up off the mattress where I'd sunk, took two steps to the front of the cell, grabbed the bars, and began screaming, "Medical emergency! Medical emergency!" The officer who had just assaulted me returned, opened the outer door, and stepped into my cell.

"What's your problem?"

"You know what my problem is. I got a medical emergency. My head hurt."

"Listen, you're scheduled to leave Lake Butler in the morning. If you report this, I'm a take you off the transfer list and you're going to be stuck here with me. So you'd better be quiet if you know what's good for you."

THE WASP IN THE WINDOW

The wasp in the window
that once buzzed full of life.
Lies still on the sill—
face first in a crack.
I wonder how it got here—
to rest before my sight.
Wings stiff & extended—
as if still in flight.
Did it fly into a web—
while still alive.
Before dying in a cell—
with holes that resemble hives.
What happened to its barb?
Does it still reside inside?
If I squeezed it with my thumb—
will I be stung if I tried?
Does it somehow feel the sun—
everytime it rise?
Or has death taken its soul—
like it did its yellow lines?
I wish I could pick it up—
and give it a proper burial.
Even an insect's cadaver—

shouldn't be kept in confinement.
But there's a barrier between us—
that prevents me from touching.
So let poetry be the button—
to open the window that I couldn't.

· · ·

BY FLORIDA LAW, I HAD TO BE TRANS-
ferred to an adult prison. Juvenile facilities
were for adolescent criminals with youthful
offender sentences of up to six years, including probation. I had been tried for a life-
and-death felony as an adult and sentenced
to life in prison without the possibility of
parole. I arrived at Apalachee Correctional
Institution, one of Florida's oldest prisons,
in the Panhandle, near a little town named
Sneads, in June 1991. This facility has a mix
of custody levels: minimum, medium, and
closed. It has two units: ACI West and ACI
East, the latter supposedly featuring less strin-
gent custody. Not long after I'd stepped off
the prison transport bus, Mr. Maybury, an affable, heavy corrections officer, said, "Manuel,
your name, DC number, place of birth, and
birthday." Your DC number is your prisoner
identification number given to you when
you're processed. You memorize it the way you
memorize your telephone number because
you have to say it every night during count.
Mine was 518907. By now I hated being asked
my birthday: I'd say "March twenty-ninth,

1977," and the response would be "Are you sure about that?" Thirty years later, my file still states my birthday as March 2, 1977, because the deputy who picked me up from the juvenile detention center the night of my arrest made the error.

At Lake Butler I had been classified for ACI East Unit. Having inspected my file, Mr. Maybury reassigned me to ACI West because of the nature of my sentence and the fact that I was on medication: He said, "Well, you can't stay here, Ian. My fences ain't ready for you." ACI East didn't have gun towers. I was quickly processed and escorted to M dorm, at the time the west unit's orientation dormitory. M dorm, like the others, had an open-bay layout, meaning all eighty bunks were out in the open—no cells, no doors, no privacy.

As soon as you stepped through the dorm's inmate entrance, you were in the dayroom area, which had about twenty chairs, two tables, and a thirty-two-inch TV positioned above the wall directly in front of the doorway, about fifteen feet away. Another door led to the inmates' sleeping area, which consisted of about eighty bunks. If you walked through the sleeping area doorway and turned immediately left twice, you entered the bathroom area, with its white porcelain sinks and toilets. At the back of the bathroom was the shower area. I was assigned to the top bunk of a bed on the right side of the dorm. My bunkmate was a black man about fifty years old named Mr. Stafford. He drew portraits for money.

I had received a Super II radio (like a miniature boom box but with only one big speaker) in a permitted package from my mother, and as I lay on my bunk, listening to the **American Top 40** countdown with Casey Kasem one afternoon, he said a girl had written in about her relationship with a boy that had to end because she was moving to another city. She asked Casey to play "Anything for You" by Gloria Estefan to serenade her boyfriend. I felt a twinge when I heard these lyrics: "But don't even think that I don't love you/That for one minute I forgot you/But sometimes things don't work out right/And you just have to say goodbye." I thought of my mom and my guilty plea. I rolled over on my side, my back toward the grown men of the dormitory; I stared out the window and recalled another lyric of the song: "And though inside I feel like dying/You know you'll never see me cryin'."

THE WATER

Sitting on a damp blue bench.
upset by unchangeable events . . .
In the distance there's a-swish!
Farther still, there's a silent
    steel fence.
I look down where I sit.
Where there's rain gathered in drips.
I see my eyes, nose, and lips.
The breeze makes them blink,
    breathe, and wish.
The image makes me reminisce—
of a different series of events.
Where I couldn't see any of this.
Or hear the ball bounce before it . . .
Or feel the brisk breeze, at its clip.
It was just me, back and knees bent.
Looking at crimson gathered in drips.
Seeing my eyes, nose, and lips.
Asking myself—
why-are-you-doing-this?
Like a camera that clicks—
the images switch.
I return to the damp prison bench.

I see the fence, feel the wind, hear
   the swish.
I reach out and touch my face in
   the water,
I taste freedom for a moment.
And I, I appreciate it.

· · ·

THE COMPOUND WAS FULL OF MEN FROM Tampa who had read about my case. The **Florida Sentinel Bulletin,** a newspaper popular among black people, had zealously covered "13-Year-Old Black Boy Sentenced to Life in Prison." I became everyone's little brother. Some would say: "Man, if it had been a black person shot they wouldn't have given that boy all that time. You know how many people I've shot?" The men I met were largely protective of me. Sometimes people assume the worst about a situation like mine: a black adolescent around older, more mature male prisoners is going to be sexually taken advantage of. That wasn't the case with me. I made friends, attended school (there were no grades), and spent hours on the basketball court.

I felt relatively safe, at least among the other prisoners and at least compared to the chaos and violence I experienced growing up in Central Park. But now and then trouble would erupt. I remember an older guy in his forties who thought I had broken into his locker; someone had told him as much.

I had not. One day he walked up behind me, grabbed me, and punched me in my face. I wrestled him to the ground and fought with him like my life depended on it. Other inmates struggled to pull me off him. After that, I started sleeping with a weapon under my pillow, even though I never had occasion to use it. It wasn't really a knife but a piece of one of those lightning rods you sometimes see attached to the roof of buildings. The prison's maintenance staff used to sell these instruments of self-protection for ten dollars apiece.

Now and then Sundays I attended church, and one weekend that summer I elected to be baptized in the prison's chapel. Matthew 7:12: "So in everything, do to others what you would have them do to you, for this sums up the Law and the Prophets." This was the fundamental precept of the religion I accepted, the religion the institution that held me espoused and promoted. But the tension between this precept and the realities of daily life in an environment controlled by a brutal combination of deprivation and neglect on one side, and raw, unchecked power on the other, was more than I could get my mind around.

ONE DAY I WAS SUMMONED TO PICK UP legal mail. I fairly ran to retrieve it. I had been anxious to hear from my lawyer about the appeal to get my sentences overturned. Sure enough, I received a letter and some legal documents from him. I read the letter as I walked back to the dorm: Judge Manuel Menendez, Jr., had denied my motion to mitigate my sentence; he had reached his decision after considering my character. My lawyer had enclosed all the transcripts and depositions in my case and wished me good luck in getting my sentences overturned by other means.

"By other means?" I had none. I walked back to the dorm in a fury, especially angry with my mother for having encouraged me to take the advice of a lawyer who had misrepresented matters to us and had no intention of appealing my case. Did the denial to mitigate my sentence mean that any appeal on my behalf would be forever out of the question?

In a letter to Peggye I was unsparing in blaming her. She responded: "Don't try to lay that guilt trip on me, boy. If you would've had your ass home like a normal thirteen year old, instead of downtown shooting people, none of this would have happened."

CENTRAL PARK VILLAGE IS NOT THE kind of place where people expect a white Christmas. In the dead of winter there are no treetops glistening or children listening to hear sleigh bells in the snow. The last time the temperature had plunged into the thirties and snowflakes had fallen was in 1977, the year I was born.

In its usual tropical weather, we children of Central Park Village—regardless of how impoverished or crime-ridden the 'hood was—always looked forward with building excitement to Christmas Day. Grandma Betty used to go around Central Park Village every Christmas morning shouting, "Merry Christmas, everybody." It was so embarrassing. For Christmas, Uncle Alvin and Uncle

Lewis would come home, on leave from the military, bearing gifts for all of us. Grandma Linda would get me train sets, He-Man dolls. Once she even got me the Snake Mountain from the bad side of Skeletor's Island. Another year she got me an Atari. Uncle Alvin, who was stationed in Okinawa, bought a Sega in Japan and had it shipped to me—this was one of the best presents I ever got.

Now, age fourteen, as Christmas approached in Apalachee Correctional Institution, I was feeling numbed by the intensity of incarceration. The touch of Christmas spirit in jail—the dispensing of a five-dollar canteen gift certificate (the Christmas Five, as it was called) to each inmate a week before the blessed day did little to ease my longing.

My depressive mood about the Christmas behind bars prompted me to do something I had not planned, much less foreseen. Going through the discovery related to my case that my lawyer had sent after the motion to mitigate sentence had been denied, I noticed in the police report Debbie Baigrie's address and telephone number. On Christmas Eve I decided to call her, not knowing exactly what I

was going to say but knowing what I wanted
to say, which was that I was sorry for what I
had done. At Apalachee, if you were in open
population on the adult side and the compound had not been shut down, you could
walk outside and use the phone to call collect; there were also phones in the dayroom
strictly for nighttime use. You could use the
phone for fifteen-minute intervals whenever
you wanted to, or rather when one was available. There were two phones on either side of
the compound and in the middle, near the
canteen, a bank of ten—so there were ten
telephones for more than a thousand men,
meaning that traffic was always heavy. You always had to be eagle-eyed for an opportunity.

The last time I had heard Debbie Baigrie's
voice was at my sentencing when she expressed
her belief that I did not care about what I had
done to her. I was nervous. When I picked up
the phone, before dialing the outside operator, I wondered whether I should assume a
false identity, whether I should pretend to be
the officer who had arrested me or the detective who had interrogated me. Debbie knew
their names and would be more likely to

accept a collect call from them. I was making no sense though: why would law enforcement be calling Debbie collect? My fourteen-year-old mind was desperately searching for a way to ensure that I would have the chance to apologize. Something inside me said, "Ian, if you really want this to work you're going to have to tell the truth and say who you are." I dialed zero and waited a few seconds that felt like an eternity before the operator picked up.

"How may I help you?"

"I'd like to call this number collect from Ian to Debbie."

"OK, hold on."

As the telephone rang, my heart was pounding furiously. A woman picked up and said hello.

"You have a collect call from Ian for Debbie. Do you accept the charges?"

"Can you ask him his last name?"

"Sir?"

"Manuel, I'm Ian Manuel." I didn't say I was calling from Apalachee Correctional.

"Yes, I'll accept the charges."

It was then all on me: what do you say to somebody you've shot? I spoke from the heart.

"Miss Baigrie, I called to wish you and your family a Merry Christmas and a Happy New Year and to apologize for shooting you in the face."

"Ian, why did you shoot me?" she asked in a soft, tremulous voice.

"It was a mistake," I said. "It all happened so fast."

"Maybe the first shot was a mistake, but then you shot at me again. Then you shot at my friend."

I think I repeated, "It all happened so fast."

I was too young to realize how unlikely it all was, that only a uniquely special person would accept a call from the child who shot her. All I knew at the time was that I had done something necessary.

We spoke for the fifteen minutes allotted us by the prison phone. Just before it cut off, I asked her, "Can I call back?" She said yes.

I proceeded proudly to tell my homeboys at Apalachee that I had called Debbie, and they teased me: "You better leave that woman alone before you get another charge." Later on, during my intermittent correspondence with Debbie Baigrie, older convicts would say cynically: "That lady's trying to trick you to get you out of prison so she can kill your ass." For now, they looked at me with skepticism; they thought my excitement at connecting with my victim would simply blow over as a bout of craziness. Some even thought I might be lying: "You didn't call no lady you shot. What's wrong with you, boy? You always playing games."

Between my call to Debbie on Christmas Eve and February 1992, I wrote three or four letters to her about what was going on with me. I wrote that my lawyer had let me down; that I was trying to better myself as a person; that I was improving my basketball skills. For nearly two months, I waited anxiously every evening during mail call for a response, but none came. I was now resigned never to hear from Debbie again, and, with my legal options for appealing my life sentence seemingly exhausted, I began to rack up disciplinary reports (DRs) for infractions that in prison were criminalized but that on the outside would have warranted grounding as punishment or even psychotherapy. Instead, I was shoved into a revolving door of disciplinary confinement for stretches ranging from a few to thirty days. Over the next year, I would receive over thirty DRs for bad behavior, roughly three per month. Yet, as many times as I was written up for infractions, I never thought about the consequences they would bring. I didn't know any better.

THERE WERE VARIOUS LEVELS OF DISCI-plinary punishment. There was your walking DR, which meant that you remained in open population, in a position to get into even more trouble and amass more DRs, until your appearance before a disciplinary court. A classification officer and a lieutenant would then determine your guilt, whether you should be given probation, or whether your recreation time should be limited. Actual physical confinement was limited because of space. In the west unit there were only about twenty cells for more than one thousand inmates. There were times when you would be sentenced to forty-five days and you would do only a week because they had constantly to rotate inmates

in and out. That is how I was able to accumulate so many DRs: no sooner was I let out of
confinement than I was back in.

When not in confinement I was often gambling in dormitories off limits to me, incurring
even more DRs, which were clearly not serving as a deterrent. There was a lot of money
to lose or win in those games. My mom was
sending me about forty dollars a month at the
time as canteen money. I would buy a case of
shrimp soup, or a case of peanut butter cookies, and Tang. What she didn't know was that
I was gambling with the money left over.

IN FEBRUARY OF 1992, I WAS TRANSFERRED
back to ACI East Unit after spending my
first eight months in prison at ACI West. The
ACI population held many inmates I knew
from W. T. Edwards and the Tampa County
jail. Mario Gilbert, Antonio and Pookie and
Scope. Even Marquis, who had enlisted me on
the fateful day of the shooting, was there, but
on the west side in G+H dorm. I went to pay
him a visit. I snuck through a gateway that
separates the east and west compounds and

walked the short distance to his dorm. I stood outside the dorm's doorway and told someone who was entering to tell Marquis somebody was looking for him. I heard his voice and saw him through the screened windows, walking down the middle aisle. When he pushed the door open, came out on the porch, and saw me standing there, he screamed, "Jim-Jim, what's up, boy?" We hugged and he jokingly said, "Jim-Jim, you don't look like Monkey Man no more, boy." He ran into the dorm and brought out pictures of people from Central Park. Even though I had only been off the streets about a year and a half, people looked different and I was beginning to forget names and faces.

We talked for about thirty minutes. Marquis, who was only sixteen at that time, explained that he had gotten ten years, three mandatory, for the armed robbery he had been in the county jail for. He told me that his job at the prison was outside-the-gate garbage detail. He rode around on the back of a garbage truck, throwing trash bags and dumping the contents of waste containers

into the truck. His route took him to the officers' living quarters, and he told me about all
the contraband he found and brought back.

As for me, I had been assigned to work
in the main laundry room. Because I found
washing and folding clothes about as much
fun as adding and subtracting fractions, I requested schooling, which meant half day at
school and half day inside the grounds behind the kitchen, dumping swill and keeping
the area clean. The swill was kept in huge steel
bins in a freezer that sat outside the kitchen.
When the swill truck arrived, we'd walk up a
short concrete ramp, enter the deep freezer,
and tilt and roll the heavy bins toward the
back of the truck. The work was grueling. On
the back of the truck, there would be an officer with a seventy-five-inch steel pole. He
would go around to each swill bin and stab
hard and repeatedly into it, making sure that
no inmate had buried himself in an attempt
to escape.

"BOY, WHAT'S YOUR MOTHERFUCKING
problem," said the officer. I had been transferred briefly back to Lake Butler because I

had complained about pain in my wisdom tooth and was supposed to have oral surgery. With a new mindset, I wasn't the timid little kid they had beaten and humiliated at Lake Butler around a year ago. Instead, I now regarded myself as a fifteen-year-old student of prison life, stronger, more sure of myself and my ability to defend myself.

I was put in open population because I had come from an adult camp. One night in the dorm, one of the officers and I got into an argument. He told me to step into the officers' station, which was connected to an inmate dorm laundry room. And this is where inmates were taken and beaten into submission before being sent back to their bunks. Inside the station, the officer began cursing at me. To his surprise, I began cursing back.

The officer looked shocked by my response and seemed to rethink whatever his plan for me had been. He got on his walkie-talkie and called for help. Two sergeants arrived, and the officer explained what had happened. One of the sergeants looked at me and said, "Inmate, how old are you?"

"Fifteen."

"Fifteen! Man, turn around and cuff up. You ain't supposed to be on the compound no way. You trying to get all of us fired?"

As I turned around and allowed handcuffs to be placed on my wrists, I said, "I ain't no youthful offender. I come from an adult camp. I'm at ACI. I'm just down here for dental."

"It don't matter—Lake Butler policy is anybody under eighteen can't be on our compound."

Once he got me in handcuffs, the sergeant confronted me. "Boy, what is this about you disrespecting my officer?"

He pulled a quarter out of his pocket and said, "Listen, I'm going to flip a coin. Heads, we're going to beat your ass and take you to jail with a DR, or tails, we're just going to beat your ass and take you to jail."

I said, "I don't care how many times you flip it, you ain't fit to put your hands on me."

I went to K Wing in the cellblock untouched, but soon I was back in the hole for a seven-day stint.

No sooner had I returned to ACI than Marquis told me that our friend and former classmate had been killed. Marquis called me to the fence one day and said, "Jim-Jim. Patrick dead."

Patrick had come to Central Park to buy a gun from a female named Caffeine. Caffeine, not knowing the gun had one bullet in the chamber, had pulled the trigger while passing the gun to Patrick. Patrick was struck in the head or chest. Marquis said that his last words were "See, I told you, girl," before he closed his eyes and died. I reminisced about our friend. I thought about our class race when we attended Robert E. Lee Elementary and how at the start I stopped to tie my shoe only to come in second. Patrick came in first. We had joked afterward about who was the fastest. The argument was moot: he was.

Patrick and I were the same age. And now he was shot dead and I was in prison. This would be the first of many reports of the death of someone I knew as a child, each related second or third hand, the details confused— was it a bullet to the head or the chest?—all of them stark for their brevity and finality, leaving no room for indulging in grief.

.   .   .

IT WAS NOW AUGUST 1992. I HAD TURNED fifteen and was housed at Apalachee Correctional Institution. I was summoned to classification and asked to sign a consent form for an interview. Channel 10 of Tampa was doing a TV show called "Kids That Kill" and wanted to interview me. Though fortunately Debbie had survived the shooting, I had been sentenced as if she had not. That must have been good enough for Channel 10.

Debbie saw the interview, and I received my first letter from her. She was furious at my account of the crime. In a childish effort to minimize what I had done, I told the reporter, "She kept going for the gun." Debbie wrote: "I can't believe it's been two years later and you're still lying about the crime." This began a five-year period during which Debbie and I exchanged letters frequently, sometimes as often as once a month. I was ashamed that I had misrepresented my crime, but I was grateful to have Debbie back in my life.

IT WAS ALSO AROUND THIS TIME THAT I was called to Colonel Harrison's office. I had been to his office so many times that it felt like my home base. Colonel Harrison had pictures of himself hunting on the walls of his office; he used to tell me stories of his hunting trips and travels. He reminded me, in many ways, of Bob Gilbertson, because Colonel Harrison also treated me like the kid I was. He told me that he had been promoted to assistant superintendent and would be transferred to Holmes Correctional Institute; he wanted me to know. This was ominous: the man who had looked out for me would no longer be there to spring me from confinement, as he often had. I felt more alone at ACI than ever.

As it sank in that he would no longer be there to protect me, I asked, "Why can't you make assistant superintendent here?" He explained that the opportunity was elsewhere; he had to go where his promotion assigned him.

After Colonel Harrison left, whenever I went to the hole, my stay would be extended, and when I got out, staff would try me in ways they never had before. One day, after I'd served a stint, a heavyset officer assigned to the back gatehouse (where inmates were counted) saw me passing through, my property in two pillowcases.

"Manuel, I'm glad to see you out. Come down and report to work this afternoon."

It was an unwritten rule in Florida's prison system that inmates leaving confinement did not have to report to work until the next day.

"Man, I'm just getting out of jail. I ain't got to go to work until tomorrow."

"That ain't no rule, that's some inmate made-up bullshit and I'm giving you a verbal order to report to work and if you don't, I'm writing you two DRs, one for disobeying an order and one for refusing to work."

When treated unfairly, I often impulsively responded and found myself right back in solitary confinement. This time I was focused on the things I had been dreaming about during my stint: I had a package waiting for me in the mailroom, plus I wanted to go to the canteen and load up on some sweets.

"All right, sir, I'll be there."

By the time I had reached the mail room, the same officer had called the female officer there to remind me to come to work. I did not fall for the harassment. I picked up my package, returned to my dorm, and then ran off to work. When I arrived at my kitchen workstation, the same officer told me that there were enough inmates back there already and that he was assigning me to Mr. Hatchet's lawn mower squad for that day.

Previously, I would have given him exactly what he was looking for: a reason to lock me back up. But not that day. Not on my first day out.

Still, I was full of anger and took it out on the lawn mower Mr. Hatchet gave me. I ran with it full speed, pushing hard into the lawn. There was a loud boom. Fire shot out the side of the red-paneled frame and I let it go. Mr. Hatchet and the other grass cutters looked at me incredulously. Mr. Hatchet ran over to check on the lawn mower. He looked at me and said, "Manuel, what's wrong with you? You don't cut grass like that!"

The exploding lawn mower was too obvious an analogy for the anger building and always on the verge of erupting in me at age fifteen. With nothing to hold me steady, no hope anywhere on my horizon, and needing all my energy to contain my rage at the chronic insults and capriciousness of those in power over every detail of my life, I began to accumulate more DRs for "disrespect." While serving yet another stint in confinement during this period, an older boy and I got in an argument in the shower that led to an exchange of blows.

AT DISCIPLINARY COURT, I PLED GUILTY to the DR but asked the officers to sentence me to a concurrent thirty days so I could get out in time for Christmas. They told me to step out of the office while they deliberated.

After a few minutes, they called me in and told me I had been given thirty days disciplinary confinement. When I saw the yellow hearing worksheet, I noticed that neither the concurrent nor consecutive sentencing box had been checked.

"I need y'all to check a box so I can get out for Christmas."

The male classification officer said robotically, "You have fifteen days to appeal our decision."

When I repeated my request, Sergeant Nobles reached out and with a stroke of her pen checked the consecutive box, before tearing off the carbon copy to give me. I could not bear the thought that I was not going to make it back to open population for Christmas. As she slid the carbon copy across the table to me, I turned around and was walking out as she yelled behind me, "Manuel, come back here and get your papers!" I kept walking as if she hadn't said a word.

She rushed in behind me. "Manuel, didn't you hear me calling after you to get your report?"

Unable to contain the pain and anger, the disappointment and outrage—this one small thing that I wanted, to be out of a confinement cell on Christmas, this one small comfort so arbitrarily taken from me—I rained down a storm of curses and insults on the officer standing, dumbstruck, before me.

Shaken, she turned from me, and walked quickly back to the hearing room. For this, they recommended that I, age fifteen, be remanded to another facility for close management. Long-term solitary confinement awaited me at Union Correction facility. The solitary confinement of children is a form of torture routinely practiced by the American correctional system. As the American Civil Liberties Union puts it:

Humans are inherently social animals; we crave community and connection with others. Being deprived of it can anguish even the most independent individuals. Solitary confinement—the practice of isolating people in closed cells for 22–24 hours a day, virtually free of human contact, for days to decades— violates this fundamental need, causing extreme suffering.

People in solitary confinement descend to a psychological and emotional state that is deep and dark. The "hole," as solitary is often called, is an apt description. Even when a person is freed from solitary, its effects may not go away. Research has shown solitary confinement causes serious, long-term harm, which is why courts across the country recognize that it should be used only sparingly, even for adults serving years in prison for violent felonies.

For children, solitary confinement is especially dangerous. Because their brains are still developing, children are highly susceptible to the prolonged psychological stress that comes from being isolated in prisons and jails. This stress can inhibit development of parts of the brain—such as the prefrontal cortex, which governs impulse control—causing irreparable damage. In other words, children subjected to solitary confinement are forced into a hole so deep they may never be able to climb out.[1]

A few days before my transfer, Marquis was released from his own confinement. He had heard that I wasn't coming back to the compound and was awaiting transfer to a close management facility. On his way out, he stopped by my cell and reached through the bars so we could embrace. As I released him, I saw tears in his eyes. We both knew—and couldn't even begin to imagine—what awaited me.

6

IMAGINE THAT YOU, AT AGE FIFTEEN, HAVE been sentenced to social death, life without parole, in a space nine feet by seven—the size of a freight elevator—where for twenty-two to twenty-four hours a day you are trapped; where in a deadly daily routine you sleep, wake up, shit, piss, eat—food slipped through a slot as if you were an animal; where you are denied the possibility of human contact except as physical or mental abuse; where visual and sensory stimuli—the stuff of life—are only a memory or a dream; and where who you are is defined only by your willingness or unwillingness to be disciplined and punished. Imagine life without hope in a brutal hellhole of sameness designed to break your spirit and challenge your sanity. The United Nations considers solitary confinement for more than fifteen days torture. It was my condition for eighteen consecutive years. Scientists have shown that solitary confinement, especially of juveniles, can damage the brain, provoking panic, anxiety, depression, loss of control, and even suicide. I managed to endure it and survive.

As early as the mid-nineteenth century, the writer Charles Dickens denounced the barbarism of the practice when he visited a prison in Philadelphia: "I believe that very few men are capable of estimating the immense amount of torture and agony which this dreadful punishment, prolonged for years, inflicts upon the sufferers, and in guessing at it myself, and in reasoning from what I have seen upon their faces, and what to my certain knowledge they feel within, I am only the more convinced that there is a depth of terrible endurance in which none but the sufferers themselves can fathom, and which no man has a right to inflict upon his fellow creature. I hold this slow daily tampering with the mysteries of the brain to be immeasurably worse than any torture of the body."[1]

The tampering with the mysteries of my own brain by prison authorities was aided and abetted by psychiatry and pharmacology. From the start of my incarceration I had trouble sleeping because of anxiety and was prescribed medication that sometimes worked and sometimes didn't. Soon, in response to my behavioral liabilities as they saw them, psychiatrists were quick to diagnose me as suffering from a form of mental illness, bipolar II disorder, which develops during the teenage years. Like bipolar I, it's characterized by a fluctuation of moods high and low, but its elevated moods—hypomanic episodes—are less intense than bipolar I's full-blown mania, and depression is its more characteristic state. But I have never suffered extended periods of highs and lows, so I have always been skeptical of this diagnosis. Bipolar depression and attention-deficit/hyperactivity disorder can sometimes be confused, though, because they share symptoms. I am certain that— because of my inattention, hyperactivity, and impulsivity—I've suffered from ADHD since childhood, but ADHD was not at the time recognized as a form of mental illness by the Florida Department of Corrections.

It is a curiosity that a state-funded institution, run by professionals, would systematically place human beings in the most toxic of settings and then, when this made them sick, conclude that the problem was coming from inside of those human beings. There is likely no diagnosis that accurately captures the range of harm and its consequences for the mind and body of someone subjected to solitary confinement. The diagnoses given to me and the drugs used to bring them under control all seemed ultimately aimed at keeping me there longer.

Among the psychotropic drugs used to treat me, or forcibly injected into me—to put me at ease for management—were Benadryl, Remeron, Depakote, Sinequan, Geodon, Seroquel, Abilify, Tegretol, Vistaril, Valproic, lithium, Trilafon, Ativan, Thorazine, and Zyprexa—regardless of their onerous and sometimes debilitating side effects. In short,

I was a constant object of pharmacological experimentation, at times shackled spread-eagle on a bed, the objective being to render me insensate, to nullify me with mind-altering drugs.

EARLY ON, I HAD LEARNED FROM OLDER inmates that you could now and then get relief from the savage sameness of solitary confinement—the feeling that the walls are closing in on you—through a change of scenery. All you had to do was shout, "I'm going to kill myself," and so initiate a psychiatric emergency. Guards would rush to your cell, strip you of your clothes, and take you to the infirmary, where they would lock you in a cold room with a concrete bunk for three days at a time. I have a vivid memory of sitting naked in such a room, shivering on a stainless steel toilet, hugging myself for warmth, my chin slumped on my chest, as I drifted off.

I later learned from a book that the origins of solitary confinement can be traced to a Quaker prison experiment at the Walnut Street Jail in Philadelphia at the end of the eighteenth century, which aimed to do away with corporal punishment and to rehabilitate offenders by completely isolating them from human society. As the **Solitary Watch** blogger Mary Hawthorne notes, solitary confinement was "ironically and perversely, a reform attempt, based on the notion of 'penitence' (hence 'penitentiary') conceived by the Philadelphia Society for Ameliorating the Miseries of Public Prisons."[2] Inmates at Walnut Street Jail were isolated in their cells to do assigned work and read the Bible with a view toward repentance. Whenever they were led from their cells, hoods were placed over their heads to prevent them from knowing where they were and from seeing other inmates. In less than fifty years, solitary confinement would become a terrible mode of punishment, recognized by the U.S. Supreme Court as inhumane. Its aim was no longer to foster rehabilitation.

AT MARTIN CORRECTIONAL INSTITUTION, inmates were stabbing each other with regularity throughout the overpopulated compound. Things got so bad that the prison started gassing inmates for surreptitiously talking to each other on the cellblock. For me solitary confinement early on was curiously a blessing—it kept me out of harm's way. I wasn't stabbed and I wasn't gassed. When I was first committed as a teenager, I spent a lot of time fantasizing, stuck in a time warp, from 1990 to 1992, when I was full of dreams. I wanted to be a superstar professional basketball player, rapper, or actor. I thought of being arrested the summer after I'd completed seventh grade. I was looking forward to eighth grade; I envisioned playing basketball for the junior high school team, the Madison Mustangs. Even though I was small, I was athletic. Would I have made the high school team? Would I have played college basketball? Would I have landed in the NBA? Might I have become the next Allen Iverson, the next Michael Jordan?

Most children's dreams are tested by the realities of their expanding world as they grow into adulthood. They learn that they will not be Michael Jordan, or president of the United States, and they find where their true talents lie. My dreams remained untested, as my world had shrunk to a cell.

I recalled the raps and poetry that I wrote while serving time in juvenile detention, sharing them with my homeboys and reveling in their encouragement. I thought that if I could deeply affect these young men, who came from tough circumstances and were hard to reach, I could move audiences outside of prison. My hero was Tupac Shakur, who rose from poverty to worldwide fame as a rapper and actor. For me he was extremely influential. Everything about him—his take-no-shit attitude, his dignified demeanor, the power of his rhymes—appealed to me. I was as much astounded by his first album, **2Pacalypse Now,** as I was by his acting debut in the movie **Juice,** about the trials and travails of four young men in Harlem dealing with the harsh realities of inner-city life. I wanted to be the next Tupac.

Once a week the library cart would come around. Inmates from the general population working in the library would bring you books that you had requested. I was drawn to gritty, hard-edged stories about the black urban experience that celebrated criminal swagger and bravado. My two favorite authors were

Iceberg Slim (**Pimp: The Story of My Life; Trick Baby; Long White Con**) and a writer Iceberg Slim profoundly influenced, Donald Goines (**White Man's Justice, Black Man's Grief; Black Gangster; Street Players**). Both career criminal writers were hugely popular in prisons at the time—their books were a snap to read—and both remain popular among rappers today for keeping it "real," for championing thug life.

SOLITARY CONFINEMENT THROUGHOUT Florida is a complex, infernal, multitiered affair. According to the Florida Administrative Code, "close management" is "the confinement of an inmate apart from the general population, for reasons of security or the order and effective management of the institution, where the inmate, through his or her behavior, has demonstrated an inability to live in the general population without abusing the rights and privileges of others."[3] Florida, the third largest prison system in the country, is at the vanguard of the mass incarceration of black Americans. Whereas black people constitute less than 20 percent of Floridians, they amount to nearly 50 percent of the state's prison population, and 60 percent of inmates under close management are black. Yet in some important respects Florida is indiscriminate in assigning offenders to close management: it is heedless of age, developmental disability, or mental illness. Even children and juveniles in state prisons can come under close management.

There are three levels of close management housing: CM 1, CM 2, and CM 3—ranging from most to least confining. Assignment to one or another supposedly depends on your record and behavior. In CM 1, offenders are imprisoned alone in around sixty square feet for twenty-two to twenty-four hours each day. Solitary confinement in CM 2 and 3 may involve a cellmate, compatibility not guaranteed. Good behavior supposedly earns greater freedom, leading eventually to integration in the general prison population. While CM 2 and 3 are said to offer more leniency than CM 1—participation in work and educational activities outside of your cell—prisoners in these categories are often denied privileges they are due. All CM 1 inmates are at the mercy of corrupt or vengeful corrections officers who, with a false or petty disciplinary report, can either retard or void progress.

A vicious cycle often ensues when prisoners who find it impossible to conform to behavioral expectations are condemned to solitary confinement: the restrictiveness reinforces and heightens their malady, resulting in the inevitable lengthening of their stay. For eighteen years, I was such a prisoner. The longer I was in solitary, the harder it was for me to meet their behavioral expectations. And the harder it was for me to do as I was told, the more forceful the prison became in attempting to ensure that I did. Looking back, I know that it is a universal human experience during adolescence to seek to assert independence, to insist on defining one's own personhood. In the context of a solitary confinement cell, this stage of my life was received as defiance and met with brutal force aimed at crushing it. My journey through the arbitrary and cruel CM system was that of the rider of an elevator that is out of control, ascending and descending seemingly with a mind of its own. No sooner would I seem to be completing a six-month sentence in CM 2, on my way to CM 3, for example, than I would find myself, after, say, five months and twenty-nine days, guilty of an infraction, real or concocted by corrections officers, that prevented me from achieving greater freedom.

Over the course of my incarceration, as I was shuttled back and forth among prisons throughout the state—Lake Butler, Apalachee, Martin, Union, Columbia, South Florida Reception Center, Florida State Prison, Santa Rosa, Suwannee Annex, Charlotte, Northwest Florida Reception Center, and Hillsborough—I amassed more than two hundred disciplinary reports. Most fell into the category of disobedience or disrespect of officials.

IN 1996 PRINCETON POLITICAL SCIENTIST John Dilulio sparked widespread social panic when he put forth a novel theory about juvenile delinquency—which he has since retracted given how stunningly wrong all of his predictions turned out to be—sounding an alarm about the advent of a "new breed" of black inner-city youth whom he called "superpredators." "Fatherless, Godless, and jobless," they are "radically impulsive, brutally remorseless youngsters, including ever more teenage boys, who murder, assault, rob, burglarize, deal deadly drugs, join gun-toting gangs, and create serious disorders."[4] This was the media landscape in which an interview with Debbie Baigrie ("I Forgave the Guy Who Shot Me")[5] was published in the now defunct **McCall's** magazine.

Debbie described the excruciating toll my crime had exacted—the shooting had ripped up her mouth and gums, requiring years of painful reconstructive surgery. But with dignity and empathy, she added:

> [A] glimpse of Ian's bleak life made me reflect on my own circumstances, the reasons I have to be thankful: a husband with a good job as an electrical engineer, a great family, a beautiful home, many caring friends. So, hoping I could make Ian's life a little better, I began a correspondence with him. My husband didn't approve. "Forget him!" Stephen said. "He can just rot." . . . It would be

wonderful to end this story with the news that Ian has been completely rehabilitated. But reality is seldom so neat. What I am grateful for is that Ian seems to be finding himself, that I have not only recovered but have been able to develop a relationship with my attacker and that I have found a new direction for my life. I still get a lot of pressure to stop bothering about Ian, but he needs a friend. And for reasons I don't fully understand myself, I intend to go on being that friend.

From 1992 to 1995 Debbie and I wrote to each other perhaps as much as once every other month. From 1995 to 1997, the frequency slowed to once every three or four months. By then Debbie had carved out a successful career for herself as a nonsteroidal bodybuilder and personal trainer, which she regarded as therapeutic, and of course she was busy raising her two daughters and running a bodybuilding magazine. It is hard for me to remember in great detail my letters from Debbie over the course of six years; with the exception of a few, they were all destroyed in a prison fire. I can recall only bits. I remember her caring, motherly tone best: she was always imploring me to stay out of trouble and encouraging me to study for my GED/ High School Equivalency exam. For my part, I wrote of teenage matters as I had read about them in magazines, and of my need to get out of prison so that I could pursue sports in college. I asked her if she could send me copies of **Sports Illustrated** and **People** that she had lying around her house, but prison policy prohibited that, fearing the slipping in of contraband.

Debbie's caring for me was shown by her willingness to drive two and one-half hours each way from her home in Tampa, on the opposite coast of Florida, to visit me at Martin; she knew that no one had come to see me in prison in nearly six years. Her request was sharply denied. A letter sent to her by a Department of Corrections functionary dated May 8, 1996, said in part: "This is in response to your letter and phone conversation requesting a visit for Ian Manuel. While you have been quite clear in your interest to help Ian, I am hopeful you can understand the position of the Department of Corrections. It is the policy of the Dept. not to permit visits by those persons known to be victims of those who are incarcerated. Such permission would not be in the interest of security, in maintaining care, custody and control of the system."

In 1996 after the **McCall's** article appeared, **The Maury Povich Show** got in touch with Debbie. It wanted to devote a full hour to our story; it wanted to have her on the set and to interview me via satellite. She told me they said that if I stayed out of trouble for thirty days I would be allowed to do the interview. She was adamant that I keep my nose clean. I explained to her that I was in the most restrictive confinement, CM 1, and that, regardless of good behavior on my part, there was no way Martin Correctional Institution was going to permit my appearance on the show. I made the mistake of telling older convicts what had happened, and they poured poison in my ears: they claimed that she was being paid for the interviews she was doing. "Boy, that lady's using your dumb ass to get rich. And here you in prison broke." Debbie was righteously offended, indignant at being the object of my suspicion when I challenged her, asking for money: "I have forgiven you for shooting me in the face, and now I'm going to forgive you for slapping me in it. And that's where it ends."

Debbie had previously considered cutting off our correspondence—before the **McCall's** article, before the Maury Povich invitation. She had reached out to my mother, presumably to bond with her, and things had not gone well. In a letter from April 1995, she wrote:

Dear Ian:
     I just got off the phone with your mother, and it was a very bad idea to call her. You see, I have been trying all this time to help you and I never realized that all of you think I should be dead. I wasn't the judge that put you in there. I was the victim. As the victim I tried to get you rehabilitated before you went to prison and have been fighting for you ever since. Only because I really care. I tried to

explain that and she sees it differently.
I think all she sees is some rich, blond
girl that couldn't begin to understand
her situation. I'm far from rich but I do
have children and I believe they need
attention, guidance and love. I always
felt sorry for you because it was beyond
my understanding why someone that
young could be with a gun. I felt you
were a victim too . . . I don't need her
approval or understanding, but I also
don't need her contempt. Right now,
I'm scared . . . No one has ever wanted
me dead before. You didn't. You didn't
even know me. She doesn't appreciate
anything I've done and I'm scared Ian!
I really am. I think I must just forget
about this . . . You are a special guy
and I believe that everything will
work out.

All the best,
Debbie

I've really enjoyed corresponding with
you. Good luck, Ian. My thoughts are
with you always.

. . . .

ON JUNE 8, 1996, I WAS SITTING IN MY cell at Martin staring ahead; I had a cellmate at the time, a guy named Terry. I was on run-around status, which meant that now and then I was allowed to leave my cell to retrieve supplies at the officers' station to hand out to inmates, and today was supply day. The cell door clicks open and I see the officer in his booth waving me over. I get dressed and join the other runarounds, grabbing stuff: toothpaste, soap, toilet paper. I lunge for some toothbrushes.

"What are you doing? You ain't passin' out nothing today, you're comin' with me. We need to take a walk."

Inmates aren't supposed to go beyond the small area near the officers' station without being handcuffed, shackled, and chained, and here I was walking free in prohibited spaces with Sergeant Adams. An improbable thought raced through my mind: was I about to be released from CM on some technicality?

"Where are we going?"

"To the chaplain's office. Anyone in your family been sick lately?"

"My mom."

"OK."

The walk felt much longer than it was; the distance between confinement and the chapel was only fifty yards or so. There, before a black chaplain, we sat. In a deep, calm voice, the chaplain said: "Ian, I got a call from your brother. I must regretfully inform you that your mother, Peggye, has passed away. I verified it with the hospital where she died." The chaplain allowed me to call Sean, who confirmed that AIDS had put an end to our mother's life. She had for a while been sending me alarming pictures of herself with her letters. She'd been a big woman, five foot four, 220, 230 pounds. Now she was getting skinnier and skinnier. I had been mentally preparing myself for the inevitable, but the fact was still devastating. She had written me to say that in her present condition she had to smoke her medication through a pipe. The disease was rapidly eating away at her. On May 31, a week and a day before she died, I was able to place a call to her from confinement—a privilege accorded to runarounds. She told me not to call again until her birthday, June 19.

June 8, 1996, was the saddest day of my life. For the very first time I felt truly alone in the world. With my mom gone, I had no one I could depend on unconditionally. I was scared in a way that shook me. My grief was bottomless. In a stupor, I was led back to my cell. Terry wanted to know what was going on. I didn't answer. I resented his presence; I didn't want anyone around. In the darkness, I curled up in bed and sobbed.

I later learned that Aunt Kathy, my mother's dear friend, and my brother, Sean, had gone to Debbie Baigrie's home to tell her the news. Debbie wrote to express her condolences; she observed how much my brother resembled me even though he was much bigger. For the next three years, she and I fell completely out of touch, our friendship in tatters. Or so it felt. Six months after my mom died, Aunt Kathy and Sean visited me to fulfill a deathbed promise to my mother. It was the first time in six years of incarceration that I had visitors who were either family or family friends. According to Aunt Kathy, my mom could never bring herself to visit me in prison because she felt the thought of leaving without me unbearable. I didn't know what to make of that.

IN 1997, AGE TWENTY, I WAS TRANSFERRED back to Union Correctional Institution, even though the facility still offered no educational opportunity—the reason for my having been transferred from it years earlier. I wrote to the Tallahassee Central Office of the Department of Corrections to say that I was eager to improve myself through schooling. For reasons I knew nothing about, Florida's secretary of education and a colleague visited and assured me that if I stayed out of trouble for six months, I would be sent to a correctional facility where I could attend school. Having complied, I was sent to Columbia Correctional Institution nearby and assigned to less restrictive CM 2.

The deal I had made with the Central Office was that I could study and learn at Columbia only as long as I avoided disciplinary charges. But Columbia turned out to be a far more brutal and oppressive place than Union; it was an entirely different kind of prison. At Columbia, lights were kept on 24/7 as a way to disorient prisoners and keep them in check—a form of torture. There, guards were dousing prisoners with chemical agents, gassing them, for even minor infractions. I couldn't stand it—even though I myself was not victimized. I had to get out of there, I had to get back to Union. So I purposefully caught three charges. But I hadn't banked on Columbia's recommendation that I be put on CM I upon returning to UCI.

I appealed to Union's close management board by telling the unvarnished truth; the board couldn't dispute anything I said. "Listen, I want y'all to check my record. I came to UCI January 1993, check my record. I've never gotten a disciplinary report here. I caught those disciplinary reports at Columbia strictly to get back to UCI. I'm home now. You don't have to worry about me getting in any trouble. Check my record." They did.

"Why is it that you can stay out of trouble here and nowhere else?"

" 'Cause UCI's home. I growed up here. I'm comfortable with the surroundings. You don't gotta worry about me here."

. . .

ON NEW YEAR'S EVE THAT YEAR THE OF-
ficer on duty opens all the food flaps on the
confinement wing, as an act of generosity.
Though he wasn't cool, he was trying to be
friendly, to create a festive mood. He lets us
shout out to each other, pass cookies around,
fill our shampoo bottles for water gun fights
through the flaps. Officer Thomson was a
big ol' country boy, black and about six foot
seven, 290 pounds. When I spot him on the
wing I squirt him. He says: "See now, Jim-
Jim, I got something for you." He gets a mop
bucket full of water and proceeds to douse
me and whatever is in my cell, including my
sheets—cupful by cupful. Quickly he closes
the flap and locks it so I can't get back at
him. As my cell door faces the officers' station wing, I shout through its crack: "Jeff,
man, come on back, lemme go out there and
change my sheets." "All right, Jim-Jim," he
says, but forty-five minutes or so go by and
he's not back.

Peering through the crack, I see a red-
haired officer trying to open the door to the
booth. "Hey, Officer," I call, and he walks
over to my cell instead. No sooner do I start

to explain what I need to do—change my wet sheets—than another officer in the station hurriedly beckons him back. A few minutes later, Officer Thomson arrives and lets me out of my cell.

"Jeff, man, it's New Year's Eve, let me call my people as long as I'm out here."

"All right, you can use the phone."

I call Aunt Kathy collect to let everybody know I'm OK and need a little money. I tell her to tell everybody to come visit me. Everything's copacetic. At the time I'm on CM 2—and because Union Correctional has no CM 3, I expect at last to be released from solitary confinement and join the general population, having completed six months of good behavior. When I hang up, CM 2 runarounds ask Officer Thomson for permission to use the phone. He lets them. I go back to my cell and fall asleep. I wake up; it's New Year's Day; everything's good: it's my month to get off solitary. You usually get your recommendation papers the first week of the month. Something goes awry: I hear I've gotten a disciplinary report—and start hearing rumors that so did the runarounds—presumably for unauthorized use of the phone. But how could this be? Inmates can't just walk out of their cells to make phone calls whenever they want. There must be some mistake or misunderstanding.

The red-haired officer who had come over to my cell on New Year's Eve, a trainee, was not supposed to be on the wing by himself. The officer who had called him back to the station had instructed him on how to justify his unexcused presence on the wing and how to falsify a DR. The trainee now claimed that I had threatened him, that I had said: "Hey, man, my cell is wet. If you don't let me out this cell to get a mop, I'm a kill you the first chance I get." Spoken or written threats, especially against officers, are among the most serious infractions in prison, so serious that they can put you on CM 2 or even 1 as punishment. Initially, to my distress, the disciplinary board recommended CM 1—no possibility of joining open population any time soon for me. I appealed to the board's inspector; I told him the truth, about the actions of the white corrections officers that night, about the phone calls—but I pointedly left Officer Thomson out of it. After his investigation, the board rescinded the false DR but not in the way I had hoped.

"Manuel, you never threatened that man. So we're not gonna put you on CM 1. We're gonna keep you on CM 2 with a ninety-day review to see if you'll be eligible for CM 3, which we're initiating. In only ninety days you'll be on CM 3 if you behave yourself. Congratulations!"

I looked at them as if they were insane. Before the false DR I was headed for open population because no CM 3 existed and I had completed the required six months of good behavior to move up to a freer level of incarceration. A trainee had lied about me, which the board acknowledged. And my reward was what? The prolongation of my solitary confinement?

This is a system elaborately constructed of rules and regulations, a bureaucracy trudging along under the cumbersome weight of its own intricate and painstakingly defined terminologies and distinctions. The consequences for failing to comply with this dehumanizing array of mandates were excessive.

But, for me, the worst part was the way in which they were so arbitrarily enforced, the way they didn't seem to reward "good behavior" but instead seemed to only encourage an alternation between outrage and hopelessness at the bizarreness of it all.

ONE DAY IN 1998 I GOT A LETTER IN THE mail; the envelope was slipped through the crack of my cell door. It was from Jimmy Reese, my father. If a letter included money, the amount was stamped on the envelope, standard practice, and this one said "$50." I knew that, like Grandma Linda, Jimmy Reese couldn't read or write, so someone must have written the letter for him. It said in part: "Baby, I know your momma gone and I just want to make up for all the years of I wasn't there for you and to do anything I can to help you. Here's 50 dollars. Tell me what you need." I had not seen, heard from, or thought about my father in nearly a decade. He had been absent from my trial and sentencing. His letter came out of the blue. I was elated, grateful, but puzzled. What or who had moved him to reach out to me now, nearly two years after my mom's death? I didn't dwell too much on all this, though, because I was most eager to tell him what I wanted. I wrote back saying: "I don't hold it against you for not being there all these years. What matters is that you're here now." I included a list of newspapers and magazines allowed by the prison; I asked for subscriptions to **USA Today; Florida Sentinel Bulletin,** an African-American publication; **People;** and **Sports Illustrated.** I also begged him for books of stamps—trading currency behind bars. He gave me an allowance of ten books per month, the equivalent of a hundred dollars. And he kept it up until late 2000, the year of the millennium.

It turned out that Jimmy Reese, now more than likely in his late sixties, was an old drug dealer. Crack. One day police tried to ram into his home, and he fired shots at them through the door, missing. Firing at police was tantamount to an immediate death sentence; it was a wonder he didn't die at the scene. I learned from his letters to me, written by strangers, that he was tackled and handcuffed, dragged off to jail, and later charged with attempted murder. The charge for some reason was reduced and he ended up receiving two and a half years house arrest and six and a half years probation. By now he was very sick; I know he went to the hospital with fluid in his lungs. Communication with him soon became a thing of the past. In 2004 a chaplain informed me that Jimmy Reese's probation officer had called to say that my father had died out of state. I surmised in Georgia, where he had relatives.

THE LAST TIME I SAW MY FATHER WAS THE next time I saw Debbie Baigrie. I was twenty-three. I had not seen Jimmy Reese since I was a child; I barely recognized the elderly black man sitting in the courtroom. Debbie and I had not seen each other since 1991 at my sentencing; we had not heard each other's voice since 1992; and we had not communicated since 1997. Both Jimmy Reese and Debbie Baigrie were at my resentencing hearing on June 29, 2000.

The year before I had bought a tattered and torn copy of the 1989 edition of Florida Rules of Criminal Procedure; I think it cost

me about five packs of cookies. I read it carefully and came across an item plainly stating
that life in prison is a maximal sentence. You
cannot sentence an individual to life in prison
without the possibility of parole and add life
probation. In addition to such a sentence
being absurd, it is illegal. So in 1999, through
Tampa public defender Max Reinhold, I
filed a motion to have my sentence corrected.
Eight months later I was remanded to Tampa
for resentencing.

Aunt Kathy gave me Debbie's telephone
number and I called her. When she answered,
there was a chill in her voice; she sounded
understandably as if she had moved on. I
told her that I had a court appearance and
wanted to know if she could be there to
support me. I had planned to present the
McCall's article as evidence of her forgiveness. She said she knew all about it—the
prosecutor had called—but, no, she was unable to come; she was going to be out of town
that day. She wished me good luck.

At the resentencing hearing,[6] I turned to
look at the audience before taking my seat.
There was Aunt Kathy and a black man I

supposed was Jimmy Reese, my father. There also was a white woman I imagined to be Debbie with a girl I took to be her daughter. At one point during the proceedings the prosecutor Donna Hanes told the judge that she expected both victims of my crime to be present but that only one wanted to be heard. The man who accompanied Debbie to her car that night, the man who my friends and I had victimized, spoke against any change in my sentence. Debbie did not speak against a sentence change and allowed my public defender to present the **McCall's** interview as evidence of her forgiveness and willingness to allow me to have a second chance at life. Aunt Kathy vouched for me, and then my father moved me with his powerful brevity: "I just say, Judge, have mercy on my son. I figure he done did enough time for the crime he had committed. I beg your honor please let my baby come home." The Honorable William Fuente agreed my sentence of life without plus life probation was unlawful and wrong. He vacated the life probation ruling. "I will adjudge you guilty and I'll sentence you to forty years Florida State Prison to be served concurrently with the sentence served in counts one, two, and three. Giving you credit for all the time previously served on those three counts to be given to you on count four . . . I wish you well."

Though Judge Fuente's ruling did not immediately change my life in any way, it had important ramifications down the road.

7

IN JULY 1999, FRANK VALDEZ, AN INMATE on death row at Florida State Prison for killing a corrections officer during an escape attempt, was killed by nine prison guards. Armed with stun guns, they bum-rushed his cell and stomped him to death (the autopsy would show boot prints on Valdez's skin, in addition to broken ribs). According to inmates who witnessed the crime, the corrections officers first dumped Valdez's body in the hallway, cleaned his cell with bleach, dragged his body to another cell, and then placed an emergency call. The Department of Corrections' first story was this: Valdez had committed suicide by plunging headlong from his bunk to the concrete floor. Prosecutors, on the other hand, claimed Valdez had been murdered to prevent him from divulging facts about inmate abuse to the press. All nine officers were either acquitted at trial or had their charges—second-degree murder, aggravated battery, battery on an inmate, and official corruption—dropped. The Department of Corrections, however, dismissed them for falsifying reports and using excessive or unnecessary force.

At the time of Frank Valdez's murder, death row inmates were warehoused in cages measuring nine feet by six, twenty-four hours a day, seven days a week. No air-conditioning or fans abated sweltering summer humidity and heat that often reached the nineties. This, in addition to the savagery of the prison guards, would spark a failed hunger strike five years later. The relief sought by the prisoners evoked not only their plight but also long-standing conditions promoting misery and suffering allowed by the Florida Department of Corrections. The prisoners' demands ranged from the mundane (the ability to purchase eight-inch plastic fans to withstand summers) to the righteous (security cameras to document the use of chemical agents against prisoners and polygraph tests for both the corrections officer and the inmate following any officer-on-inmate physical assault).

WHEN I ARRIVED IN MARCH 2000, THE atmosphere at Florida State Prison, "the Green Monster," was tense, dangerous. Instead of physically brutalizing inmates for infractions serious or petty, real or not, corrections officers were gassing them with impunity from a distance. I was transferred to FSP.

After I was kept on CM 2 in the wake of the investigation that had vindicated me, I simply could no longer tolerate the shit. Everything that I had been holding back gushed out. I started verbally abusing these corrections officers with a sense of purpose. Gone was whatever willingness I had left to conform to such rules as making my bed military style. Gone was whatever inclination I may have had to heed orders barked at me as if I were subhuman. I was unable to bite my tongue when addressed without respect, which pretty much meant all the time. They would stare maniacally at me as if I'd slapped them in the face, so accustomed were they to brokenhearted obedience by their charges. To make matters worse, Officer Thomson was busy lying about me to my fellow inmates, suggesting that during the investigation I had ratted on him and them. He went around falsely claiming that I had told the investigator that he had let me out of my cell and allowed the orderlies to use the phone. "Jim-Jim in there tellin' them everything, how the cigarettes get in, how y'all used the phone. He all up in your shit."

Officer Thomson was calling me a snitch—not an insult I could take lightly. Such an accusation could be deadly behind bars, putting me at risk of attack from any number of inmates and guards. In my mind Thomson and I were now mortal enemies. But before anything further developed, I was transferred from Union Correctional to Florida State Prison.

IT'S ONLY A FIVE-MINUTE DRIVE ACROSS A short bridge from Union Correctional

Institution to Florida State Prison—home of the state's electric chair and lethal injection bed—where you can smell evil in the air. My Haitian friend—a big black man named David "Duplex" Jerome—Albert "Q" Quinn, a couple of other inmates, and I arrived in a white van that made its way through the back gate of the prison to the fabled long black steel ramp that leads to a doorway of FSP's second floor. Over the years I'd heard stories of how it was customary for a posse of guards at the back ramp to welcome chained and handcuffed prisoners with a reputation for unruliness at other institutions by beating and kicking them all the way up to the doorway. Luckily, we avoided this fate. Inside, we were registered and hustled to the medical bay for quick exams, then down a long hallway to our assigned wings.

There are thirteen wings at FSP: B, C, D, E, F, G, H, I, J, K, L, M, and Q. Every wing has three tiers. Every cell is a single. Locked in a cell as hot as lava in summer and cold as ice in spring, you are left to your corrosive thoughts and imagination. Back then, no female officers worked the hallway; no female staff were permitted to walk it without a male escort. Access to a wing was through a big steel door with a double lock—one inside and one outside. Two or three Officers worked as turnkeys every shift. I was placed on K Wing, where there are approximately ninety cells, thirty per floor, cells facing each other. I was on the first floor in the middle of the left-hand side of the wing. Each cell had a bunk, small shelf, vent, toilet, sink, and a long, deep metal footlocker. Each cell also had a back window with a wire screen that could easily be ripped, enabling an inmate to fish through the bars for contraband or to engage in other illegal activities. Through the window you could also see the green grass below and the adjacent wing. Prisoners would often communicate with each other through their windows; they would engage in one-upmanship, trying to "shoot" (silence) their opponents with witty insults, playing their own version of the dozens.

IN MY EARLY TWENTIES, WHEN I WAS AT FSP, my learning expanded, thanks largely to some convicts I befriended who had been in prison for twenty-five years or more. The books they recommended sometimes spoke more to their condition than to mine. As men who had been incarcerated in the 1970s, they regarded themselves, no matter their crimes, as political prisoners of racist America to one degree or another. So books such as **Soledad Brother: The Prison Letters of George Jackson,** by the Black Power revolutionary, and his memoir **Blood in My Eye**—completed only days before he was killed in 1971 by San Quentin prison guards while allegedly trying to escape—were akin to their Bible. I had never politicized my confinement; I always took it personally. Their conversations about books of egocentric, unconventional morality, such as Robert Greene's **The 48 Laws of Power,** and Ayn Rand's **Atlas Shrugged** and **The Fountainhead,** were heady stuff, supposedly with vague implications for my plight—though I found some of the reading difficult to plow through. My taste ran from the mammoth postapocalyptic novel **Swan Song** by Robert McCammon—the longest book I had ever read cover to cover—and the first two books of the Harry Potter series, **Harry Potter and the Sorcerer's Stone** and **Harry Potter and the Chamber of Secrets.** I was drawn to fantasies that gave my imagination flight, fantasies about a final struggle between good and evil to determine the fate of the world. Since those days a line, often quoted by one convict I knew, has stayed with me: "To live is to suffer; to survive is to find some meaning in the suffering."

IN 2002 OFFICER THOMSON, HAVING BEEN transferred from Union Correctional Institution to Florida State Prison, found himself working on the wing that I was on. One day I was in my boxers sitting in my cell waiting for the nurse to bring me medication. Late at night my mind would race; I needed medication to grab and relax it so I could hit deep sleep. Instead I heard the clinking of the gas chain somewhere outside my door. This infernal device is like a fire extinguisher with an extended hose, and it has a distinctive sound that lets you know when the gas is coming. I didn't know what was going on until Officer Thomson and Sergeant Dougal got to my cell's flap. I heard Officer Thomson laughing, letting me know outright that he hadn't forgotten the bad blood between us. He sprayed me with a chemical agent through the flap. The kind of gas they used on me was clear; the heat it generated on my shirt-less body was intense, fiery. It was as if I were standing in front of an oven blasting, its door open. I couldn't get away from the pain for hours. I had to move constantly to lessen the hurt however slightly.

When my body cooled, the heat of my rage took over. Looking back even now, I'm still not sure how I was supposed to go anything but crazy in that moment. Brutally terrorized at the hand of state employees, with no pos-sibility of recourse, no one to come to my aid. I was reduced to my most basic elements, fighting for my very existence, my most basic sense of dignity. I lost myself. I lost any hope I would ever go home, ever leave this prison. In my fiery rage and despair, I would immo-late myself—literally. I wrapped myself in newspaper and set myself on fire. Thomson was forced to come to my cell, to witness what he had done, the lengths he had pushed me to. In my deepest of hopes and despairs, I would tackle him, take him down with me. But the officers only put the fire out and restrained me. They cuffed and chained me up, and hauled me off to the showers where I was forced to stand under the running water for hours. I was eventually dragged to the medical bay to have my wounds dressed and then to disciplinary confinement—administered by, among others, Officer Thomson.

It was at this juncture that the toll of long-term solitary confinement would begin to be felt most acutely and self-destructively. My life had shrunk to the size of an eight-by-ten cell. And my preoccupation became defending that cell and the shadow of the life remaining to me. Within that space—both physical and mental—I turned on my own body and began cutting myself, as I saw numerous others in confinement do.

BLOOD, IT SEEMED TO ME, WAS THE ONLY thing respected in Florida State Prison. Inmates commanded attention by spilling blood, either their own or others'. Cutting was prevalent among them; cell walls were scrawled with blood denouncing this or that. I had learned that prison guards would let you bleed to death in your cell unless you forced blood under the door, where a camera would see it—so I learned to do this.

"BLOODY MIRROR"

Imagine someone trying to kill you
But you don't know who they are.
Every time they touch you—
You see another scar.
You try to run away—
But they always run you down.
And leave you with your blood—
Falling to the ground
You hate whoever does it
With overflowing passion . . .
You can't see who it is . . .
You can't see through the tears—
Surrounded by the blackness . . .
Sometime during the struggle
Your blood begins to puddle
Until reflective like a mirror
You clearly see why you have suffered
When you looked into the blood.
The image took your breath.
Because the person trying to kill you
Was nobody but yourself.

. . .

BEGINNING IN 2002, I KEPT A FRAGMENT of razor encased in a salt packet in my mouth everywhere I went, as a protective measure. I convinced myself that prison guards would never be able to put me in a situation from which I could not extricate myself. If they forced me into a freezing strip cell, for example, all I had to do was cut myself and they'd give me a blanket. When I was a child I once was wrestling with a friend in the backyard when suddenly he let go of me and my head hit a wall, injuring an area right above one of my eyes. I was rushed to the hospital, where my wound was sewn up. Time and again I cut precisely along that scar to bleed.

ONE DAY, HAVING BEEN PLACED ON SUIcide watch, I was standing on the sink in my cell talking to another prisoner through the vent when an officer walked by, tapped the door, and told me to get off the sink. Usually what they did was gas you when they caught you talking. But because I was on suicide watch, their rules didn't allow this. The officers had their own way of handling this, usually by denying food. But I refused to beg, to plead for nourishment. They had taken all they were going to take from me.

When mealtime came and nothing was slid through my flap, I destroyed the sprinkler in my cell. It poured in my cell, drenching me, water rushing through the crack at the bottom of the door. The officer demanded that I cuff up or he would call the cell extraction team. Things always get extremely ugly with the cell extraction team. By now I am mentally exhausted and emotionally numb. Five prison guards arrive, dressed in riot gear. They lined up one behind the other, their hands on each other's shoulders. The lead man holds the shield in front of him—I remember hoping it would be the plastic and not the electric one. I counter with the wet mattress from my bunk to protect myself against the inevitable onslaught and to cushion my fall when they would pummel and wrestle me to the floor. They drag me to medical, where they put me in four-point restraint. All the holding cells were full; so they swap one inmate out for me and tie me down.

. . . .

ONE DAY A RAY OF SUNSHINE SHONE
through the darkness of my life. I was led
from my cell to take a legal call. Because of
the motion to correct a legal sentence that I
had filed in 2000, I had been appointed an
appellate public defender named John C.
Fisher. He was now calling to say that he
had filed a writ of certiorari that had made
its way to the U.S. Supreme Court, arguing that a fourteen-year-old should not have
been sentenced to life without the possibility of parole because it was cruel and unusual
punishment. Certiorari is a judicial process
seeking review of a decision by a lower court.
The Supreme Court had ordered the state of
Florida to reply.

He was excited, joyful. "Ian, I've filed these
petitions before and the court has never asked
the state to respond. I think we got something here, man. Keep the faith."

A few weeks later he informed me that
Florida had responded to the petition and the
Supreme Court had dismissed the writ. He
said he was sorry; he had done all he could

do. He hoped that I would file for clemency and he wished me good luck.

"DON'T NEVER LET THEM TAKE YOUR mind," my mom had told me when I was a boy, and that became my mantra for survival. But this required staunch discipline: both unconscious and conscious repression of all manner of pain. The death of my grandmother, the death of my mother, the death of my father: the accumulation of loss weighed on me every time I was beaten, every time I was gassed, every time I lost an appeal. As a young man growing up, you learn that real men don't cry. This is reinforced exponentially in prison. You can't show signs of weakness; you can't cry. Otherwise they'll know what they can do to harm you. If you acknowledge the damage they are doing to you, they'll keep it up. So you push things down so as not to feel the pain. But beware the repressed: its return always comes at a cost. In T dorm Crisis Stabilization Unit, I was given short-term care, during which acute psychiatric syndromes, as expressed by mood and anxiety disorders, were diagnosed and treated. I refused medication, resulting in yet another disciplinary report against me.

BY 2005 I WAS A TWENTY-EIGHT-YEAR-OLD who had spent roughly half his life in prison— and most of that in solitary confinement. I was living an absurdity, serving a forty-year sentence concurrently with a life sentence without the possibility of parole. My anger had so deepened that I was no longer trying to get off CM. The intensity of my fury scared even me. I was back at Union Correctional Institution, in U dormitory, and one day I was led to medical for a call out. When I returned to my cell I saw that all of my property had been tossed. Prison guards had searched it for I don't know what: painkillers, ibuprofen? So I tore my mattress open and set it on fire, oblivious to the consequences. Officers rushed to put the fire out and pillaged my cell. I had kept my personal effects—pictures of my mother; letters from her, Debbie, and my brother; and other irreplaceable objects of sentimental value—in my locker. They raided it and threw all its contents out, as if to erase whatever past I may have been clinging to as a human being. They lied; they said the fire had consumed it all. For the next thirty days, they tried to break me. Every time I was let out of my cell—to visit the nurse, to talk to a counselor—I was forced to wear a spit shield and some kind of black box strapped to my back; my feet were shackled. A chain, a leash, was attached to the handcuffs slicing into my wrists behind me, as I was commanded to walk.

Time expanded infinitely in my cell. Somehow I had managed to secure pen, paper, envelopes, and stamps. I attacked the formal grievance process; I spent whole days firing off grievance after grievance to functionaries at the Department of Corrections and others in the legal profession about how the prison was treating me.

IN 1999—THE YEAR FRANK VALDEZ WAS killed—Mark E. Osterback, a prisoner at Walton Correctional Institution in Florida and fourteen other inmates who had been subjected to close management (CM) filed a class action complaint against Michael E. Moore, Secretary, Florida Department of Corrections, and wardens throughout the state's prison system.

Its preliminary statement powerfully denounced the degradations of close management:[1]

1. This is a class action for declaratory and injunctive relief alleging that the Defendants house inmates assigned to Close Management under conditions so harsh, atypical and punitive as to amount to Cruel and Unusual Punishment in violation of the Eighth Amendment to the United States Constitution.

2. The conditions under which Close Management inmates are housed result in serious mental and physical deterioration.

3. The conditions under which Close Management inmates are housed pose a danger to the public since a large, although unknown number of inmates complete their sentence while on Close Management

and are released directly from Close
Management to the street.

Among the suit's major allegations were
these:

204. The effects of Close Management
on the plaintiffs, and the Class they
represent, are profound. Placement
of prisoners with serious mental
disorders on Close Management
exacerbates their underlying mental
disorders, induces psychosis, and
increases the risk of suicide or other
self-inflicted harm. Even mentally
healthy prisoners are likely to develop mental illness after placement
on Close Management.

205. Due to their mental disorders, some
Class members never leave their
cells, even to shower.

206. The restrictions imposed on inmates in Close Management are
so punitive, atypical and harsh
that they violate the Cruel and
Unusual Punishments Clause of the

Eighth Amendment, made applicable to the states by the Fourteenth Amendment.

Responding to the complaint, in an offer of judgment, the Florida Department of Corrections agreed in 2001, "without liability," to implement certain remedies:

In order to minimize potential harmful effects of close management housing, Defendants have developed a Close Management Consolidation Plan, the key components of which include the following:

1. Reduce the number of institutions that house CM inmates from ten to four (one for females and three for males), to consolidate security, program, and mental health staff resources; and to facilitate more uniformity of program operation;

2. Conduct staff training on mental health issues relevant to the CM population;

3. Perform mental health screening before and after CM placement to help ensure timely access to necessary mental health services;

4. Assess behavioral risk for each CM inmate, in order to provide more objective information that will be useful for mental health and other service planning, as well as for administrative decision-making (e.g., modification of CM level or termination of CM status);

5. Provide full range of outpatient mental health services (e.g., group/ individual counseling; case management; psychiatric consultation; psychotropic medications; and timely referral to inpatient care), commensurate with clinical need, as determined by the Defendant's mental health staff;

6. Provide self-betterment/stimulation programming to CM inmates.

Only two years later, the Department of Corrections sought to terminate the Order of Judgment, claiming its remedial goals had all been achieved to everyone's satisfaction. This brazen attempt to avoid responsibility for a disgraceful state of affairs resulted in the reopening of the discovery phase of the trial and the scheduling of an evidentiary hearing in September 2006. I was one of thirty-one prisoners and experts who testified. Attorneys for Osterback et. al. (the plaintiff) had searched Florida's penal system for witnesses to the horrors of close management. I, regarded as "a poster boy" for having served more time on CM than anyone else, and other prisoners—from FSP, Charlotte, Santa Rosa, and Lowell—were invited to Union Correctional Institution to testify via satellite. The video was transmitted to open court in Jacksonville, where Federal District Court Judge Henry Adams was presiding. I told the judge I had been in solitary confinement since I was age fifteen. I told him about the first time I cut myself. I pulled bandages off my arms and legs to show the fresh wounds currently on my body. In late August, I had slit my wrist and the nurse closed the wound with superglue before sending me back to my cell. I spoke of how solitary confinement had led to my "decompensation" ("a breakdown in an individual's defense mechanisms resulting in progressive loss of normal functioning or worsening of psychiatric symptoms," according to the dictionary of the American Psychology Association). I explained that, before solitary confinement, I had never hurt myself intentionally, but now I did so once a week with any sharp object ready to hand—a piece of metallic toothpaste tube, a tiny shard of glass.

"DOES SEPARATION EQUAL SUFFERING: Some state inmates spend years in solitary. Critics say that is cruel and unusual."[2] This was the headline of an article by Meg Laughlin that appeared in **The St. Petersburg Times.** It centered on my testimony and was altogether empathetic. The Department of Corrections would have none of it. Assistant State Attorney Jason Vail told the newspaper: "These prisoners don't practice civilized behavior. They don't follow rules. They don't deserve civilized treatment. It's a different world." A few days later he called the paper to clarify his remarks: "What I meant to say was that these inmates don't conform and are there because they don't follow the rules. It's that simple."

8

"FREEDOM'S JUST ANOTHER WORD FOR nothin' left to lose," the song says. From around 2003 to 2010, I was free in solitary confinement. I was inured to it; I had adapted to the hellishness of my environment. As Guitar says to Milkman in **Song of Solomon:** "You wanna fly, you got to give up the shit that weighs you down." I did.

The prison system, as I saw it, was engaged in nothing but an all-out assault on my soul. It wanted me to cower before its rules and regulations, holding out rubbish as enticement. It said to me: "We're going to treat you like shit, lower than a human being, and you're going to take it gleefully for the privilege of our releasing you from close management to open population. We're going to burden you with unfairness: you must put up with eighteen months of insane rules. You can behave yourself for five months and twenty-nine days, trying to get out from one CM level to a more lenient one, but if on the thirtieth we write up a disciplinary report against you, justifiably or not, you'll have to repeat six months." Many inmates were willing to make that deal—to get back to their lovers, to be able to play basketball or watch TV. I grew to see these concessions as tools of mind control. I refused to succumb to the savagery of the prison system's official violence. So fuck the recreation yard; fuck basketball; fuck TV.

IN THOSE DAYS, ARM-BREAKING BY COR-rections officers—authorized by the chief of security—became common practice. Whenever a prisoner had a problem or a dispute—he wasn't fed or had a medical emergency—he would more often than not take the cell door flap hostage by placing his arm on it, preventing its closure, until the officer on duty spoke to someone in charge or the matter was resolved. Colonel Whitehurst judged this act to be a wanton violation of prison protocols, tantamount to an assault, and gave permission to any officer in such a situation to grab the inmate's arm, hold it aloft, and slam the flap down on it. Prisoners unaware of the rule and commandeering the flap— "I need to see the captain"; "I need to see the nurse"; "I've got a medical emergency"; "I wasn't fed last night"; "I need to go to group therapy"—were fodder, their screams chilling as they realized what was happening.

During these years I cherished my aloneness in solitary confinement. I was rarely bored. Boredom in addition to the intensity of the incarceration would have made me lose my mind, might have driven me to suicide. I spent hours on end imagining, practicing magical thinking. Suppose the ocean is a fantastical realm. Posit two aquatic animals: on the one hand, a swordfish whose large gills pull more oxygen out of water than those of most fish, allowing it to spend its entire life beneath the surface of the sea; on the other hand, a dolphin or a whale, with its diving reflex, which however long it stays submerged must periodically rise to the surface to breathe air through its blowhole because like humans it has no gills. In prison, an inmate who never emerges from fantasy and delusion may be said to have slipped into schizophrenia, having completely withdrawn from reality. An inmate who dives deep into his imagination but is compelled for his survival now and then to rise from fantasy and delusion retains a firm grip on things as they are. I have always believed that I was of the latter party.

Most of my time I spent swimming in my imagination. I had a constant vision of my mother, at the feet of God seated in His throne in heaven, imploring Him: "Please let my baby go home." I wrote rap lyrics to express my ever-shifting feelings; read poets like Langston Hughes, Maya Angelou, and Eminem, imagining myself in competition with, and trying to outdo them; longed for visitations from the nurse just so I could see a female form on the wing. I dwelled on what life would be like outside prison, what I would do once I was out. I harbored childhood fantasies of becoming a rich and famous rap star. I would give back to those I had left behind in prison. Powerless as I was, I dreamt of wielding it. I would hire lawyers—they like money—to represent the interests of prison inmates and to abolish close management.

"MANUEL!" THE OFFICER KICKED MY CELL door, rousing me from a reverie, sometime toward the end of October 2006. "Get up, you got legal mail. Come sign for it." I got up from my bunk and walked the three steps it took to get to the cell door. The officer opened the food flap and placed a piece of paper on it. I signed for the mail and he gave me the envelope and walked off. I studied the envelope; the letter was from an organization in Alabama. What could they possibly want with me? I didn't know anybody in Alabama. I tore the envelope open; God had sent me a gift, I thought.

Equal Justice Initiative
Of Alabama
Mr. Ian Manuel
DC # 518907

Union Correctional Institution
7819 N.W. 228th Street
Raiford, Florida 32026-4000

Dear Mr. Manuel:

I'm the director of a non-profit law
firm called the Equal Justice Initiative
in Montgomery, Alabama. We have
a staff of attorneys who provide legal
representation to people in prison. We
have primarily handled death penalty
cases for the last twenty years. However,
we recently began a project providing
legal assistance to individuals who have
been sentenced to life imprisonment
without parole as juveniles. After the
U.S. Supreme Court's decision in
Roper v. Simmons (2005) banning the
death penalty for juveniles, we started
working on the cases of prisoners
who were sentenced to LWOP at a
young age.

In identifying young people
sentenced to life imprisonment without
parole for offenses committed at age
14 or younger, we spotted your case. We

believe that there may be a chance to reverse a sentence of life imprisonment without parole under an analysis that flows from the **Roper** decision and wanted to know if you were interested in meeting with us to discuss this possibility.

As you know, post-conviction litigation is very time-sensitive with lots of procedural defaults and statutes of limitation that can bar review of claims. We are also limited in how many cases we can take on. However, a distant review of your case suggests that we might be able to offer you some legal assistance if you're interested and will get in touch with us quickly. We are a non-profit organization and do not charge anyone we represent a fee for the legal assistance we provide.

If you do not currently have legal representation and would like to discuss obtaining assistance, I'd like you to please call my office at 334-269-1803 as soon as possible. In addition to practicing law, I am also a law professor

at the New York University School
of Law and am frequently out of the
office. If I'm not available, please speak
with Aaryn Urell or Rebecca Kiley, who
are attorneys working on this project.
If you are not able to call our office
because of restrictions placed on you by
your prison, please write us immediately
and we will make arrangements to try
and meet with you at your prison. We
look forward to hearing from you soon.

I enclose some additional information
about our project with this letter and a
return envelope in the event you cannot
call us and need to write in response to
this letter.

All the best to you.

Sincerely,
Bryan A. Stevenson
Executive Director

After reading Bryan Stevenson's letter, I was
at once elated and skeptical. Two years earlier,
I had written to Al Sharpton's National Action
Network, the ACLU, and Jesse Jackson after
learning of their interest and involvement in

the case of Lionel Tate. (I had requested their addresses from the prison law library.) In 2001, Tate was sentenced to life imprisonment without the possibility of parole for severely injuring Tiffany Eunick. The twelve-year-old boy said that he had been imitating wrestling moves he had seen on TV on the six-year-old girl, who died from her injuries. In 2003 an appeals court overturned Tate's conviction and paroled him. Given that the victim of my crime had survived and now supported my eventual release, I thought Sharpton, the ACLU, and Jackson might advocate to overturn my sentence. If memory serves me correctly, only the ACLU responded, and it was more concerned with mounting a class action suit than challenging my sentence. One year later, in 2005, a Florida State University law professor contacted me offering to come to my aid, only to dash my hopes and dreams by deciding not to take my case. Something about Bryan Stevenson's letter seemed different, genuine, more intimate. It asked me to call or write; I decided to do both. I persuaded the dorm lieutenant that I needed to make a legal call. My hands were cuffed in front of me and I was taken to the nurses' station supply room. Handcuffs jangling, I dialed the numbers on the letter. I closed my eyes and silently prayed that Bryan would be there. "EJI," a woman answered. I told her who I was and that I was calling to speak to Bryan Stevenson. "I'm sorry, Mr. Stevenson is busy right now; may I take a message?" I looked down at the letter and thought quickly to ask: "Are Rebecca Kiley or Aaryn Urell in? Bryan told me to ask for them if he wasn't available." The secretary put me through to Aaryn.

"Aaryn speaking."

"Ms. Urell, this is Ian Manuel calling from a prison in Florida. I received a letter from your organization telling me to call, and you'd send some lawyers down to see me."

"Excuse me? Sorry, Mr. Manuel, but we're a small law firm in Alabama. And we mostly deal with death row cases in Alabama. Are you on death row?"

"No, but I received a letter from your executive director. And he promised to send lawyers down to see me if I called."

"What's the name on the letter?"

"Bryan Stevenson."

"Hold on."

As I waited, smooth jazz wafted through the receiver; the song was "Like a Star" by a young British R&B singer being celebrated everywhere, it seemed. The lyrics were all too appropriate: "Just like a star across my sky/Just like an angel off the page/You have appeared to my life." I looked over my shoulder and saw the lieutenant, his face pressed against the window. He was losing patience and mouthed: "Hurry up, Manuel." I shouted angrily: "Man, they got me on hold." The officer stared at his watch and signaled with his hand that I had five minutes. My response to him was cut short by words issuing from the receiver.

"Hello, is this Ian?"

"Yes."

I was moved by the calm friendliness of the voice: "This is Bryan Stevenson, how are you?"

The first words out of my mouth weren't about his letter, the law, or lawyers, but about the song I had just heard.

"I'm fine. Was that Corrine Rae Bailey I was listening to while on hold?" Mr. Stevenson corrected me in a sweet, fatherly way: "Ahh, Corinne Bailey Rae. She's quite a talented artist. How do you know of her?"

"I read about her in a magazine recently," I replied. I wanted a connection with this man beyond the fickle attorney-client relationships I was used to. I asked him about the letter he had sent. Was he serious about assigning attorneys to my case? He assured me that he was. He asked me a few questions: How old was I when I committed the crime? Did I currently have an attorney? By now the lieutenant was banging on the window and yelling: "Time's up, Manuel. Time's up."

"The officer is saying I have to go."

"Don't worry. EJI attorneys will visit you in the next couple weeks."

"You promise?"

I was so used to being disappointed and lied to by lawyers I was desperate for confirmation before hanging up.

"I promise."

ONE THING ABOUT BRYAN STEVENSON: HE is a man of his word; when he tells you he is going to do something, he follows through.

A couple of weeks after I spoke to him on the phone, two young lawyers, Rachel Germany and Irene Joe, flew down from Alabama to see me. Rachel, a light-skinned black graduate of NYU Law School, hailed from Brooklyn. Darker-skinned Irene was from Houston by way of Nigeria. Both were committed warriors against racial injustice. They told me they couldn't make me any promises. They sought to get the measure of me by verifying my age when I committed my offense and inquiring about its circumstances. Equal Justice Initiative, it appeared, was interested in representing me because I was so young when I was sentenced to life without the possibility of parole and because the crime I had committed was nonhomicidal. Rachel and Irene would report to Bryan, and if EJI decided to take on my case, they would be back with a retainer for me to sign.

They returned with a photographer in tow. You have to understand that for years I had not seen myself; mirrors were not a luxury afforded me in prison. I was eager to see how I looked and wondered whether I would recognize myself in the photos. I asked EJI for copies to send to distant family and acquaintances as proof that I was still alive.

Equal Justice Initiative sought to base its case on the unconstitutionality of cruel, and unusual punishment, which it hoped to argue before the U.S. Supreme Court—success being a long shot, hinging on a Hail Mary pass, as I saw it. Jailhouse lawyer that I thought I was, I at first quibbled with their strategy. I had spent nearly a decade and a half dealing in Florida state courts. EJI seemed intent on creating new law, which I thought would fall on deaf ears in the state. I wanted them to engage Florida law already on the books and argue manifest injustice in my case. Manifest injustice refers to an unfairness shocking to conscience, an unfairness that is direct, obvious, and observable. I wanted EJI to argue that my original plea of guilty was not knowingly and voluntarily given, that there had never been a competency hearing. On February 22, 1991, my lawyer had told the judge that there were aspects of my background that called my competency to stand trial into question. According to the law, if a defendant's competency is questioned before

the court, the judge must order an evalua-
tion, which he did in my case. But the judge
did not hold a hearing to determine my competency as required. Two psychiatrists did in
fact examine me and said I was fit, even as
they called me a sociopath—but not in an
open hearing with a declaration by the judge.

The suitability of adult sanctions imposed
on me was also questionable. There is to this
day a Florida law that says a child of any
age indicted for a life-or-death felony shall
be treated in every respect as if he were an
adult. There are criteria that a juvenile must
meet to be sanctioned as an adult; the judge
cannot simply serve up conclusionary language, offering no specific evidence related
to the criteria for transferring a juvenile to
adult dominion. The judge in my case did
precisely that. It should be noted that Florida
tries more children as adults than any other
state. As an "issue commentary" of the James
Madison Institute states: "Florida prosecutors have virtually unfettered discretion to
decide which children to try as adults. While
Florida law authorizes 'judicial waiver' [a
court hearing to determine whether a child

should be tried as an adult], more than 98 percent of children tried as adults are 'direct
filed' in adult court by prosecutors—with no
hearing, due process, oversight, or input from
a judge."[1]

THE MIDDLE-AGED BLACK MAN SITTING
on the other side of the Plexiglas barrier was
there to save my life. He wore a gray suit and
reddish tie. He was serene and soft-spoken.
His manner was professorial. On my side I sat
handcuffed, shackled, waist-chained. My blue
prison uniform hung loosely from my body.
Years of malnutrition and blood loss from
cutting gave me the look of a concentration
camp survivor. Bryan Stevenson was visiting
to connect with me human to human and
explain how his legal strategy applied to my
case, gently disabusing me of my legal pre-
sumptuousness. In 2005 the U.S. Supreme
Court had acknowledged the fundamental
differences between children and adults, and
had determined that children could not be
subjected to the death penalty because of
the Eighth Amendment, which forbids cruel
and unusual punishment. As Bryan would

write in **Just Mercy,** "My staff and I discussed how we might use the constitutional reasoning that banned the execution of children as a legal basis for challenging juvenile life-without-parole sentences."[2] He would file cases in Alabama, Arkansas, California, Delaware, Florida (mine), Iowa, Michigan, Mississippi, Missouri, Nebraska, North Carolina, Pennsylvania, South Dakota, and Wisconsin. Were any of these cases to reach the Supreme Court, resulting in a favorable ruling, juvenile life-without-parole sentences would be overturned. Bryan promised to stay in touch and send me copies of the amicus briefs filed in support of Equal Justice Initiative—prominent individuals and organizations felt what had been done to us as kids was wrong and should be corrected.

During the visit I told Bryan how in 2007 I had fallen in love with poetry and how it sustained me. Writing poetry had become a routine for me; I would spend four to five hours a day at it. Sometimes words to etch a situation would come swiftly; at other times I would struggle to find the right ones. No matter, for in either case I lived in my imagination, at once far away from and deep within the brutal realities of my condition. I found the practice healing, therapeutic—and profitable. Fellow inmates paid me to write poems for them to send to their families and lovers. As our visit ended, I asked Bryan if he would accept a gift of poetry. He said sure. I flipped through the stack of handwritten poems I had before me, searching for four I regarded as my best at the time: "Genie in a Bottle," "Pound Puppy," "Yes We Did," and "Uncried Tears." Bryan honored me by including the last of these in his book **Just Mercy:**

Imagine teardrops left uncried
From pain trapped inside
Waiting to escape
Through the windows of your eyes

"Why won't you let us out?"
The tears question the conscience
"Relinquish your fears and doubts
And heal yourself in the process."

The conscience told the tears
"I know you really want me to cry

But if I release you from bondage,
In gaining your freedom you die."

The tears gave it some thought
Before giving the conscience
   an answer
"If crying brings you to triumph
Then dying's not such a disaster."

THERE IS AN MSNBC DOCUMENTARY CALLED
**Lockup: Inside Florida and Santa Rosa
Correctional Institution.**[3] At the beginning
a deep voiceover intones: "There are more
than 102,000 men and women doing time in
the Florida State Prison system. Of the fifty-
six state prisons for men, one is considered
the end of the line, the place male inmates go
when other prisons can't handle them. The
Santa Rosa Correctional Institution, located
on Florida's panhandle." Inmates there are
considered "the worst of the worst." If you
engaged in cutting, seeking attention or special treatment, for instance, corrections officers simply ignored you. As one guard put
it, Santa Rosa inmates are there because of
"their repeated disciplinary reports in the

department, their disruption of institutions throughout the state, their disobeying orders from staff, their non-receptiveness to the correctional process as a whole." I was transferred from Union Correctional Institution to Santa Rosa in the fall of 2007, when I was thirty years old.

SOMETIME IN 2008 MY BROTHER SEAN called Santa Rosa prison from the hospital in Tampa. At first the prison refused to allow me to accept the call, but Colonel Barnes, whom I had known at Union, relented. Sean announced that he was dying; he didn't have long to live. I implored him to be strong. He said he was trying, but he was too far gone. His heart was a disaster. I asked whether he had inherited his disease, fearing that I myself might one day succumb to it: "Man, you dyin' kinda early; do I have to worry about this?" He said no; he had quickened his demise by abusing alcohol and drugs. I would be fine, he insisted, because I was in prison and didn't suffer from his addictions. Before he died I talked to him twice. I wrote a poem for him called "While There's Still Time," which I read over the phone. I forgave him for not supporting me during my incarceration. I vaguely alluded to what he had done to me as a child, and I forgave him that as well. While there was still time, I wanted to assure him I harbored no ill will. I wanted him to die in peace. Aunt Kathy would later read my poem at his funeral.

9

I REMAINED AT UNION FROM SEPTEMBER to December 2008, before being sent back to Santa Rosa. The psychiatric team at Union in charge of evaluating me—including my therapist and counselor during my previous stint there—came to the conclusion that I was fine, far from insane. "You ain't crazy. Your ass is going back to Santa Rosa," they said, even though it was not until November that they removed my spit shield—a contraption that looks like a cross between a surgical mask and a beekeeper's hat without the crown—which I had been wearing when I stepped off the van from Santa Rosa. I had never spat at anyone in my life; the spit shield was meant simply to debase and humiliate me into subservience.

. . .

THE EQUAL JUSTICE INITIATIVE HAD IN-
telligence that I was struggling, that things
were not right with me. So—in addition to
sending me canteen money for necessities—
Bryan Stevenson assigned a social worker to
assess my needs and provide constant support.
On October 22, 2008, Maria Morrison entered my life; she came to Union Correctional
Institution to visit me (she had recently joined
EJI to manage clinical and therapeutic services
for incarcerated clients as well as for formerly
incarcerated people and their families). Her
sister Charlotte was a Rhodes Scholar and had
been at EJI since 2000; she was now a senior
attorney there. Maria is herself brilliant and
well read, and at the time had already earned
three academic degrees. When we first met at
Union we were allotted the customary two
hours to talk, but I barely lasted one and a
half, even though I was struck by Maria's un-
canny attentiveness. I was in severe physical
distress: through the spit shield my breathing
was laborious; my hands were cuffed behind
my back instead of in front of me, common
practice allowing an inmate to take notes or
sign documents during a legal visit; the chains

constricting my body were so tight they cut into my kidneys. I was constantly shifting from one uncomfortable position to another. Empathizing with my anguish—appalled by my condition—Maria at one point tried to snatch the spit shield from my head, but instinctually I leaned back, preventing what would have been deemed a breach of security, possibly barring her from ever visiting me again. I excused myself by saying I had to go to the bathroom, but not before imploring her to promise that she would visit me again.

Maria returned to Union at least once a month, and we wrote to each other often. My decades-long ordeal had led me to construct nearly impenetrable defenses against the abuses of prison life, but, more important, against the notion of vulnerability. It had become impossible for me to trust anyone. Maria from the start seemed able to navigate around some of those defenses. She encouraged me, through building a connection with her to care about myself and others. In Maria I found the reliable compassion that I had been missing all my life.

Maria's dedication to me was unswerving,

even though it sometimes invited snarky, sexist comments from prison staff. This occasional unpleasantness did not deter her. She was always clear and insistent about two things: she accepted me just as I was; and she would be there consistently for me, as long as I needed her. To be clear, her acceptance did not mean we didn't argue. Maria regularly reminded me I did have something to lose now—I had a legal team who cared about me and were working to overturn my sentence. And she encouraged me to "always keep your long-term goals at the front of your mind, Ian." Over the next five years, she dutifully copied by hand sections of a GED prep book and mailed them to me to study. Of the four sections of the exam—social studies, mathematical reasoning, science, and reasoning through language arts—mathematical reasoning was my weakest subject. She sent me sample exams to study and was relentless in her instruction. Together we read and discussed books that a high school student might read, such as George Orwell's **Animal Farm** and Harper Lee's **To Kill a Mockingbird.**

Orwell's allegory about the rebellion of farm animals seeking equality against a totalitarian farmer spoke to me, especially the betrayal of the rebellion leading to the authoritarianism of the pig Napoleon. **To Kill a Mockingbird**—supposedly about racial injustice and the corruption of innocence—left me cold. I found it interminable. Atticus Finch was no hero to me; he was the paragon of a lawyer out for himself, a man of dubious integrity. I found the whole white-man-as-savior-of-black-man story objectionable in the extreme. Atticus to my mind was full of shit, like many of the lawyers I had tussled with. Maria's exposing me to a wide range of ideas, some of them conflicting, encouraged me to trust her, at first cautiously, then wholeheartedly.

I once begged Maria, while I was beginning to feel a need for spirituality in my life, a need for exploring the possibility of a larger meaning, to send me a popular psychology best-seller I had heard about (with forewords by Oprah Winfrey and Maya Angelou, no less), **The Seat of the Soul** by Gary Zukav; Jay-Z claimed it had made a difference in his life while improving his relationship with Oprah. I was a convert, or so I wanted to think, to its philosophy of the proper alignment of personality and the soul. The book became my Bible; time and again I repeated this passage whenever I confronted an especially onerous vicissitude of my condition: "Say to the universe, 'Find me and take me where you know I need to be.' Let go and trust that the universe will provide, and so it shall."

THREE YEARS EARLIER, IN 2005, IN RE-sponse to **Roper v. Simmons,**[1] the U.S. Supreme Court ruled that the Eighth and Fourteenth Amendments to the Constitution prohibited the death penalty for offenders who were younger than eighteen years of age when their crime was committed. Reaffirming the need to be informed by "the evolving standards of decency that mark the progress of a maturing society," Justice Anthony Kennedy, writing for the majority (Kennedy, Stephen Breyer, Ruth Bader Ginsburg, David Souter, and John Paul Stevens), stated: "When a juvenile offender commits a heinous crime, the State can exact forfeiture of some of the most basic liberties, but the State cannot extinguish his life and his potential to attain a mature understanding of his own humanity." The opinion added that "retribution is not proportional if the law's most severe penalty is imposed on one whose culpability or blameworthiness is diminished, to a substantial degree, by reason of youth and immaturity." Chief Justice William Rehnquist and Justices Antonin Scalia, Clarence Thomas, and Sandra Day O'Connor dissented.

It was the **Roper v. Simmons** ruling that encouraged and emboldened Bryan Stevenson and the Equal Justice Initiative to embark on a nationwide litigation project against the cruel and unusual punishment of juveniles sentenced to life without the possibility of parole—a righteous campaign against their death in prison, which was tantamount to the imposition of the death penalty. According to EJI, at the time there were only eight people in the world serving life without parole for crimes committed when they were thirteen, and all eight were in the United States. Only two had committed nonhomicide offenses, and both were inmates in Florida. Both had already spent more than half their lives behind bars: Joe Sullivan and me.

IN 1989 JOE, A SERIOUSLY MENTALLY DIS-abled thirteen-year-old boy, had been lured by two older teenagers to join them in the burglary of a home in Pensacola. Later that day, someone raped a seventy-two-year-old woman there. Lena Bruner, the victim, who was blindfolded and beaten, testified that her assailant was "a colored boy"[2] who "had kinky hair and he was quite black and he was small." Joe admitted to the burglary but strongly denied the rape. DNA evidence that might have exonerated him was destroyed before his trial and was not even requested by his public defender. One of Joe's accomplices, the likely culprit, however, implicated him in the sexual battery in exchange for a light sentence in juvenile detention. In court proceedings that lasted less than a business day, Joe was tried and convicted by a six-person jury on five counts: two each for burglary and sexual battery, and one for grand theft. Having exhibited remarkable indifference and incompetence (he barely addressed the court), Joe's public defender was later barred from practicing law in Florida. Treated as an adult when he was thirteen because he had a criminal record, and sentenced to life in prison without the possibility of parole, Joe—now a thirty-three-year-old man wheelchair bound because of multiple sclerosis—was about to get his proper day in court after nearly a score of years of prison misery—as was I.

The Equal Justice Initiative's representation of me began in 2007 with the filing of a postconviction relief motion in the Thirteenth Judicial Circuit of Tampa—a so-called 3.850 pursuant to Florida's Rules of Criminal Procedure—which seeks to vacate, set aside, or correct a sentence through a "collateral attack." A collateral attack is an attempt to impeach or overturn a judgment with factors that are not in the court record of the original action—the court record itself being the basis of an appeal. A judgment may be challenged on these grounds: it violated the Constitution or laws of the United States

or the state of Florida; the court lacked juris-
diction to impose the sentence; the sentence
was above and beyond that which was authorized by law; and the plea was involuntary.
A 3.850 had been filed on my behalf by my
public defender in 1993, but it went nowhere,
and the statute of limitations for doing so
was two years, so we held out little hope for
this EJI filing. The Thirteenth Circuit denied
the motion and we appealed for a review of
its decision to the Second District Court of
Appeal. As my case languished there, two developments unfolded that would have a profound impact on my life.

The First District Court of Appeal in
Florida dismissed EJI's appeal on Joe Sullivan's
behalf with prejudice on procedural grounds
and argued that the **Roper** decision "established only one new constitutional right, the
right for a juvenile not to be given the death
penalty."[3] The court offered no opinion on
the appeal, disallowing recourse to Florida's
Supreme Court. Its decision dramatized a
legal fact: it's easier to get a death penalty
reviewed at all levels of the judiciary than
it is a life sentence. In December 2008—

around the time I was returned to Santa Rosa Correctional Institution—EJI filed a petition with the United States Supreme Court asking it to find Joe's sentence of death in prison for committing a nonhomicide crime when he was thirteen cruel and unusual. Florida's attorney general at the time, Bill McCollum, waived his right to respond to the petition, perhaps because he deemed it without merit. But on May 4, 2009, the U.S. Supreme Court miraculously (because such decisions are so rare) agreed to hear not only **Sullivan v. Florida** but also **Graham v. Florida,** a case filed by Bryan S. Gowdy, an attorney unaffiliated with EJI.

Terrance Graham, who suffered from attention-deficit/hyperactivity disorder, was the son of crack-addicted parents in Jacksonville and had led a troubled life. In 2003, when he was sixteen, he was charged as an accomplice in an armed burglary and attempted armed robbery of a barbecue restaurant. Terrance pled guilty and, because he had neither participated in the violence nor stolen money, he was sentenced to one year of detention in a juvenile facility and three years' probation. In 2004 Graham was accused as a codefendant in a home invasion and of having held the robbery victim at gunpoint. Two years later, when he was nineteen, he was convicted of violating the terms of probation and was punished with Florida's maximum statutory penalty for the violation, life without parole. The First District Court of Appeal rejected Graham's challenge of his sentence's constitutionality under the Eighth Amendment, even as Florida's Supreme Court refused to review the case. So the stage was set for a historic day, May 4, 2009, when the United States Supreme Court would hear oral arguments for not only **Graham v. Florida** but **Sullivan v. Florida,** regarding the constitutionality of sentence at issue. Meantime, EJI filed and was granted a motion in the Second District Court of Appeal to stay the proceedings of my case until there was a ruling in either of the two relevant cases before the highest court in the land.

DISCIPLINE CONFINEMENT TIME STOPS when you are in a mental health dorm. You become, in effect, frozen in time, remaining in a solitary cell while never making progress toward being released back to open population, unless, of course, you reach the end of your sentence and are released directly to the street. Conditions in the mental health dorm at Santa Rosa had devolved from bad to worse in ways that defeated imagination, courting not only the absurd but the unconscionable.

An edict was issued for this dorm that directed officers to refrain from intervening in response to any form of self-injury. What ensued was horrible. Men in the dorm, suffering a range of mental health conditions in the worst possible settings, caused untold harm to themselves—and were left to bleed and suffer alone in their cells. The medical staff were directed to offer no anesthesia when stitching self-inflicted wounds.

"You didn't care about anesthesia when you were cutting yourself; the pain was good to you, wasn't it? So why now? Man up!" With consummate officiousness, the doctor who barred me from Q dorm said: "Manuel, you're just an inmate like everybody else. You're not going to get any special treatment; you're going to have to work your way through CM, through level 1, level 2, and level 3." Did she know that I had been in solitary longer than anyone in the state? Did she know it began when I was fifteen? Did she know I had lost my entire family in that time? Did she know someone out there still loved me? That I was someone? I was someone.

I HAD HEARD THROUGH THE PRISON grapevine who would write back to you if you sent them a letter and who wouldn't. I had written to Florida's U.S. Senator Bill Nelson a couple of years before about my criminal case. He had responded that as a federal agent he could not involve himself in a state judicial matter. In February 2010 I learned that a Cuban dissident had died in prison after a long hunger strike protesting the government's violation of human rights. I decided to approach Senator Nelson anew from this angle. As I am not in possession of the letter I wrote, I'll paraphrase its contents. "Listen, I've been in solitary confinement since I was fifteen years old. I'm now thirty-three. I've been in here seventeen and a half years, and I'm starting to decompensate. The staff are allowing me to hurt myself and not doing anything about it. All I want is the opportunity to get treatment and be released from solitary confinement, man. This is unjust. I wrote you before, and you told me that you couldn't get involved in my criminal case. But what I'm writing about here is cruel and unusual punishment, a violation of the Eighth Amendment of the Constitution. I hope you can intervene in this matter."

Senator Nelson sent my correspondence to the head of Florida's Department of Corrections, who in turn contacted the warden of Santa Rosa. The same doctor appeared outside my cell one day. She slid a document under my door—a form authorizing release of medical and psychiatric information to Senator Nelson. She wanted me to check and initial only one box specifying something or other and sign at the bottom. I refused. I was determined to check all boxes; I wanted the senator to know everything about me—my medical record, my psychiatric record, my dental record, my HIV status. When I said as much to her, she demanded the document back and walked away. Minutes later, the warden, the assistant warden, the colonel, and the woman approached my cell.

"Manuel, what's wrong with you, what's wrong with you, man?" the warden asked and then continued: "I do everything in my power, everything in my power to help you, and this is what I get?"

"You do everything in your power to help me? What are you talking about?"

"What are you writing to Senator Nelson for, telling him all this shit about how nobody wants to help you? Huh? Didn't you know you were about to be assigned to CM 3?"

"No. Since when?"

"You know, I wonder about you sometimes. And is there a reason you told the doctor you weren't going to sign the release?"

"I said I would if she allowed me to initial whatever I wanted to initial and sign."

"Initial whatever, sign wherever, let's just get this over with," the doctor chimed in, defeated.

The upshot was this: in a meeting room near Q dorm, there was a huddle including the warden, the assistant warden, the prison's head of mental health, the Department of Corrections's head of mental health (by phone), and me to chart my future. The powers that be intimated that they had done everything to break me, to make me conform, unsuccessfully, and were ready to try a different tack. They made me an offer I didn't refuse. In exchange for assuring doctors associated with the Department of Corrections at the state level that being in close management did not cause me to decompensate—in essence to say that I had lied to Senator Nelson—I would be discharged from the mental health unit, and if I breezed through CM 1, 2, and 3 in ninety days with good behavior, I would be placed in open population. Everything proceeded as planned, but after ninety days, the warden came to me to say that Tallahassee had had a change of mind.

"Ian, Tallahassee is not going for it. You've been raising hell for seventeen and a half years; ninety days of being clean is not going to do it. But here's what they're offering instead: a transfer to Suwannee. It's a brand-new prison and you'll get a fresh start there. Go there, be clean for ninety days, and they'll transfer you anywhere in the state you want to go."

In confidence, he went on, "Ian, in my twenty-five years of being an officer I have never seen an inmate write one letter and motherfuckers start jumping through hoops to please him. I don't know what you put in that letter or what you got goin' on, but you good!"

The prospect of being in open population after eighteen years of solitary confinement gave me a sliver of hope that I was closer than ever to going home, that one day I would walk out of my cell—no handcuffs, no shackles— and feel sunshine on my face.

THREE MONTHS AFTER MY LETTER TO Senator Nelson, and one week after the U.S. Supreme Court agreed to hear **Graham v. Florida** and **Sullivan v. Florida,** the following appeared in the **Tampa Bay Times:** "When he was 13 years old Ian Manuel shot a woman in the face in a botched robbery in Tampa. She lived and he got life. Manuel, now 33, has spent nearly all of his time in prison in solitary confinement, caught in an endless cycle of misbehavior and punishment. As Florida's longest-serving inmate in solitary, he has no work skills, no formal education and so much psychological damage that he once set himself on fire. People always assumed—whether he killed himself or died of old age—that Ian Manuel's death would happen behind bars. Not anymore. He may walk out of prison in the next year. The U.S. Supreme Court is considering two Florida cases that deal with the constitutionality of locking away children for life when they haven't killed someone. A favorable ruling in either case could result in Manuel's sentence being thrown out. Confronted with the possibility of his release, prison officials, who had kept Manuel as far away from civilization as they could, are scrambling to prepare him for life outside. And his attorneys are laying out a plan that will attempt to protect Manuel from a world he fears will present him with more choices than he can handle. 'The uncertainty out there makes me nervous,' he says, 'but I'm determined to succeed.' "[4]

In the run-up to oral arguments for **Sullivan v. Florida** and **Graham v. Florida** before the Supreme Court in the fall, members of the press started reaching out to me for local color and commentary. Among them was Meg Laughlin, the reporter from **The St. Petersburg Times** who had followed my case with determination and empathy since first interviewing me in 2006, and had now ferociously braved prison bureaucracy to visit me. In 2010, even as tougher punishment for youth who had committed serious crimes was increasing, while mass incarceration was in full swing, there was intense focus nationwide on the pros and cons of sentencing youth whose offenses were nonhomicidal to life in prison without the possibility of parole. An editorial in **The New York Times,** published on the very day of oral arguments, November 9, staked out a progressive position. With respect to Joe Sullivan and Terrance Graham, the **Times** concluded: "These were two very troubled children in need of adult supervision and perhaps even time behind bars. But it is insupportable to conclude, as the courts did, that children who committed crimes when they were so young were beyond rehabilitation. The laws under which they were convicted violate current human rights standards and the Constitution."[5] I wondered whether

victory for either Joe or Terrance would be
a victory for the child I had been—and what
precisely that would mean.

WHEN THE SUPREME COURT HAS MORE
than one case concerned with the same matter, it will often choose only one to adjudi-
cate or will conjoin them for a single ruling.
Regarding **Sullivan v. Florida** and **Graham v.
Florida,** the court decided to rule on each case
separately—perhaps a concession to its ideo-
logical factions—giving rise to the possibility
of different outcomes with different consequences for inmates like me. On May 17,
2010, it handed down its judgments. With respect to **Sullivan,** it took a decision that was
no decision, affirming the conclusion of the
First District Court of Appeal of Florida: "The
writ of a certiorari is dismissed as improvi-
dently granted."[6] Translation: having agreed
to hear the case, the court declined to rule
on it—largely because, as Justice Ginsburg
had intimated during oral arguments, the
challenge to the Eighth Amendment had
come too late, after the statute of limitation
in Florida had expired, and because there

seemed to have been a disagreement about **Roper v. Simmons:** was the death penalty "different" from "life without the possibility of parole," as Justice Scalia maintained?

The disposition of **Graham** was an altogether different matter. The court was clear, voting 6 to 3 for Terrance Graham; Justices Antonin Scalia, Samuel Alito, and Clarence Thomas dissented. Justice Kennedy announced the opinion of the majority: "The limited culpability of juvenile non-homicide offenders and the severity of life without parole sentences all lead to the conclusion that the sentencing practice under consideration is cruel and unusual. This court now holds that for a juvenile offender who did not commit homicide the Eighth Amendment forbids the sentence of life without parole. . . . The state need not guarantee eventual freedom to juveniles convicted of nonhomicide crimes, but it must give them some meaningful opportunity to obtain release based on demonstrated maturity and rehabilitation."[7] In his dissent Justice Thomas upbraided the majority for, as he saw it, substituting its own moral judgment for that of the American people. The man who had replaced Thurgood Marshall on the Supreme Court deemed this ruling "a mistake" that he hoped would one day be struck down.

The ruling in **Graham v. Florida** held out hope of remedy for 129 inmates across the country who, as juveniles, had been sentenced to life without parole for nonhomicide crimes—77 of whom were imprisoned in Florida, like Joe Sullivan and myself. But not only did the Supreme Court not guarantee freedom but the ruling stated: "It is for the states in the first instance to explore the means and mechanisms for compliance [with its decision]."[8] Who would determine what "meaningful opportunity to obtain release" meant? Who would assess whether "maturity and rehabilitation" had been achieved? My fate was far from certain.

10

"IT'S OVER! IT'S OVER! I'M OUTTA HERE," I kept shouting with giddy excitement as I paced back and forth in my cell on the day of the Supreme Court's decision regarding Terrance Graham and Joe Sullivan. I was in confinement in, I believe, dorm C at Santa Rosa. I owned a radio that I had somehow bought and managed to smuggle into my cell. I was an avid fan of National Public Radio then— the guards being none the wiser because I would listen stealthily through headphones.

At around one o'clock on May 17, 2010, on whatever NPR show was coming on, there was an announcement of the top stories that day and out of the blue I thought I heard "in a six to three decision, the U.S. Supreme Court overturned life sentences for juveniles"—or something like that. My mind raced. Jesus Christ! Could I really have heard that? The fleetingness of the announcement was frustrating beyond belief. I had to wait half an hour—the longest thirty minutes of my life—for an update. Now here it was: in a 5–4 decision, the U.S. Supreme Court has agreed to overturn all life sentences for juveniles who committed nonhomicide crimes. Still, only at five o'clock did a journalist analyze the decision and what it meant. The discrepancy between 6–3 and 5–4 apparently had to do with Chief Justice Roberts: even though he had written an opinion concurring with the majority—he deemed Graham's punishment to be disproportionate to his crime—he thought the court's categorical ban of life without parole for nonhomicide crimes committed by juveniles overly broad and argued that such cases should be adjudicated individually.

About a week later I got a call from EJI. Maria and Alicia D'Addario, a lawyer assigned to Joe Sullivan's case, were ecstatic to assure me that the **Graham** decision applied to me and that I should expect to be resentenced soon. They congratulated me richly. The Equal Justice Initiative appealed to the Second District Court of Appeal to have the **Graham** ruling control my case.

By September 2010, I had not been charged with a single disciplinary report since February; I was determined to stay on the straight and narrow to comply with the Santa Rosa warden's stipulation that if I kept my nose clean I would be transferred to Suwannee, the new prison, where, if I continued to conform to expectations, I would earn the right to be sent to a prison of my choice. Suwannee was at first all I imagined it would be; it was a good camp where abuse of power was not a constant theme. The warden there was getting ready to retire the following year and wanted to keep things on an even keel. His attitude was "Let's run this place exactly how it's supposed to be run, so we won't have no problems."

DURING THOSE THREE MONTHS, AS I FO-cused intensely on making sure I remained disciplinary-report-free, something happened that nearly derailed my hopes. It concerned, of all things, poetry. When I arrived at Suwannee, I was given a job as an orderly. I passed out food trays, cleaned the dormitory—chores like that. I was on the least restrictive level of control management. I was assigned to meet with a therapist monthly while at Suwannee. Therapy relationships in prison are not what they are in the free world. You are asked to share your deepest feelings and thoughts with someone who reports to the administration tasked with imprisoning you. Letting your guard down can lead to punishment, as I was reminded during this time of change and hope in my life. Beginning to imagine my life ahead of me, my hopes for all the things we all hope for—a home, fulfilling work, security, love—I was writing a lot of poetry. Lulled into a sense of comfort with my therapist, I shared one of my poems with her. Moved by the poem, she asked if she could have a copy of the poem, and I gave her my clean draft. My therapist shared the poem with her supervisor, who came by herself to see me a few days later.

"Ian, what are you doing? You're about to get off CM; you can't be writing poems to my staff."

"What? What are you talking about?"

"The poem you wrote can be considered an attempt to establish a personal relationship with a staff member. You know what that means—sixty days in confinement—don't you? If I write you up, you won't be getting off CM anytime soon. Tell me why you did this."

I didn't think I had done anything wrong; in my mind the poem was just one of many I had written. I do find it curious that, as strong as my memory is, I don't remember the title of the poem nor do I know it by heart as I do so much of my writing. Perhaps I was too distracted by the trouble the poem stirred up to take the time to memorize it. The hoopla over the poem—the warden was apprised of it—happened in late October or early November, ten days or so before I was to appear before the CM review board. I was haunted by my past: every time I had been on the verge of getting off CM, something would happen that would prevent me from getting off. Oh shit, I thought. Not again?

Sitting before the CM review board, I heard for the first time in eighteen years, "Ian, we're releasing you to open population." My therapist and her supervisor had declined to make a ruckus about what I had written. I couldn't believe the words I had just heard. Was I dreaming? Had my mind finally yielded to a fantasy? Do you know what it's like to wait on something for so long you think it will never happen—and then it does all of a sudden? I grew increasingly nervous; I was desperate to get to the compound to prove to myself that life in open population was indeed my new reality. But procedures had to be followed before I got there.

After the CM review board hands down its decision, you are visited by a state classification officer, who has the power to approve, modify, or deny the board's decision. So if the CM board had, for instance, decided to send me back to CM 2, the state classification officer could have said no, let's keep him on CM 3. He is the final arbiter 95 percent of the time. The officer eventually made his rounds, stopping by the cell door of each inmate who had appeared before the CM board during the past week. Getting off CM means that you have the right to be transferred to a prison of your choice for good adjustment. When the official reached my cell door, he inquired where I wanted to go. He ran down a list of institutions; I chose Everglades CI, near Miami, because I didn't like the sound of some of the other available prisons.

A COUPLE DAYS LATER, SOMETIME BE-tween eight and nine o'clock in the morning, there was a knock on my door. It was the dorm's lieutenant.

"Hey, Manuel, get up and get dressed; somebody wants to talk to you."

I do as I'm told and walk out of my cell—because I'm on CM 3, I'm allowed to leave my cell unshackled as long as I remain in the dormitory. But the lieutenant escorts me downstairs leading to the quad's front door (you are not supposed to go beyond the front door without being handcuffed and shackled if you are a CM inmate). I recall the walk to the chapel in 1996—nearly fifteen years earlier—when I was told that my mom had died. I have no one else to lose now: not only my mother but both my grandmothers, my brother, and my father are all dead.

"Where are we going?"

"Somebody wants to talk to you."

I find myself in the warden's office. He is there and so is the assistant warden.

"Ian, congratulations! You did it, you got off CM. The classification officer has signed your papers. But we had to stop your transfer to Everglades CI. We're gonna keep you here with us on the compound."

"Whoa, hold up, hold up! That ain't the deal I was promised. I appreciate everything y'all done for me. Thanks very much and all that, but I was told that if I did three months on CM 3 at Santa Rosa clean, I would be transferred here; if I did three more months clean at Suwannee, I'd get to pick whatever prison I wanted to go to. I was gonna choose someplace close to home. The classification officer didn't seem to know anything about that deal, so I chose the best option from the prisons he listed."

"You're from Tampa and that ain't nowhere close to Miami. We're gonna keep you here, which is closer to Tampa, and if you do three more months here clean in open population we'll transfer you to wherever you wanna go."

"All right, man."

I now understand the bait and switch to be a Department of Corrections modus operandi, but what choice do I have? They order me back to CM dorm to pack my stuff. They release me after lunch when count clears.

MY VERY FIRST REACTION TO BEING IN open population was nothing I could have anticipated. As soon as my ID was activated, I bum-rushed the canteen, intending to eat in a single day all kinds of foodstuff I had been denied for twenty years, from honey buns to little microwavable chicken sandwiches. My canteen account had grown: most of my money—in addition to the money Maria sent every month—was from strangers who had read Meg Laughlin's article about me, sympathized with my plight, and wanted to keep in touch. You weren't allowed to spend more than sixty-five dollars per week in the canteen, but with the holiday season approaching another ten dollars was added to the limit. I was overwhelmed by the kaleidoscope of provisions. I wanted everything.

"How much are those Ritz crackers?"

"That's expensive shit, man, two dollars and twenty-five cents. Nobody buys them."

"Well, I'm going to."

At the dorm assigned to me—half of which was reserved for inmates in open population and half for inmates in confinement—I met Detroit, an old-school player, a sharp inmate with a seriously messed-up eye who had just come back from court, where he was suing the Department of Corrections for what had happened to him at Florida State Prison. Power had gone out; the place had gone dark. In the belief that the prison's cameras were disabled, guards had jumped Detroit and beaten him to a pulp. But it turned out that the cameras were working fine; the prison had a backup generator. Detroit promised to look out for me and show me the ropes in open population—a blessing, for the scene had to have changed in the twenty years since I was last in it. At first blush my early days in open population were a blur of gambling, dreadful poker player that I was. I got back into Georgia skin, while betting on football and baseball. Directly, Detroit taught me something about spending money that I still remember to this day: everything going out and nothing coming in equals zero.

One day he and I were coming back from chow, and as we passed the captain's office near our dormitory, someone in it who had been trying to start a basketball league for inmates asked Detroit if he wanted to be the compound's "basketball commissioner." Detroit said no, leaving an opening for me brashly to volunteer. "Shit, I'll do it." I had no idea what I had signed up for, even what the first steps should be. Detroit helped me to build the league and organize a tournament; he was my bracket man. We went from dorm to dorm to let everybody know that teams needed to be formed and named. The Miami Heat—of K or L dorm—proved to be the best. I assigned a time and a scorekeeper—and even someone to sweep the basketball court.

What I appreciated most about my job was the freedom of movement it allowed.

I remember shouting a Lil Wayne lyric as I strolled the compound: "I'm so official all I need is a whistle." Some inmates would tease me: "You already have a whistle, commissioner," referring to the one that proudly hung from my neck. Sometimes even officers would get in on the act: "Ain't no game today, so why you walkin' around with that whistle?" The whistle became my talisman; it made me feel important, more consequential than ever before.

IN LATE NOVEMBER, I WAS TOLD TO PACK up my belongings; I would be going to Tampa. I was immediately elated, imagining that I might be headed home at last. But then I was informed that, because the Second District Court of Appeal had handed down its opinion that the **Graham** ruling applied to my case, and assuming I was still represented by a public defender, a judge in Tampa had taken it upon himself to act on the opinion and had summoned me for resentencing. The county sheriff came to Suwannee to pick me up for the two- to three-hour drive. As the van entered my city and I stared out the window, I grew misty-eyed, recalling my early years and the disappointment of my resentencing hearing in 2000. I was placed in solitary confinement again, albeit temporarily, first in Orient Road Jail, then in Falkenburg Road—Tampa had a policy that any inmate with more than a twenty-year sentence had to be so housed. These fast-breaking developments came as a surprise to me and EJI. I was allowed to call Maria and my auntie to let them know where I was. Mark Shapiro, my EJI attorney, flew down to represent me.

At the resentencing hearing Florida's attorney general dropped a bombshell: he would appeal to the state's Supreme Court to review the Second District Court of Appeal's ruling, which, he argued, should have had nothing to do with me. The attorney general maintained that the **Graham** case concerned only juveniles who had committed nonhomicide offenses. I, he insisted nonsensically, had been charged with attempted murder, which falls under the homicide statute. To put it kindly, his position was a stretch, lacking legal basis. Everyone in the courtroom was shocked by his brazen bullshit for the sake of vindictiveness, his foolish wrangling with a decision handed down by the U.S. Supreme Court as the law of the land. I was in solitary confinement again from late November to right after Christmas—peak holiday season—which darkened my mood. I grew bitter, resentful of the state's petty vendetta against me. I was hauled back to Suwannee to await the Florida Supreme Court's ruling.

IN MAY 2011 THE FLORIDA SUPREME COURT refused to hear the case; in October the U.S. Supreme Court followed suit. But by then Suwannee had changed. A new warden was in charge—a short, bald-headed man who looked like a poster boy for Ku Klux Klan membership, and whose clear mission was to make the lives of inmates as miserable as possible. He instituted the infamous 5:00 a.m. to 5:00 p.m. rule: you had to be up and dressed by 5:00 a.m., your bed made with strict precision; you could lie down only after 5:00 p.m.; if you were caught awake or asleep in bed during those twelve hours, you would be gassed and stripped for seventy-two hours. He shut the basketball league down, depriving inmates of something to do and me of whatever sense of personal power I had cultivated in open population. A terrifying pall fell over the place. Guys with nothing to do took to drugs, especially K2, a dangerous synthetic cannabinoid, which induced, among other side effects, paranoia, psychosis, and hallucinations. Corrections officers would seize the slimmest justification to search your cell, flinging your belongings about like so much refuse to emphasize your worthlessness. You could smell fear in Suwannee now, as violence against prisoners ramped up.

One incident captures the sickening atmosphere of the place. A hulking officer—about six four and 250 pounds—was walking a little white inmate—about five three and 125 pounds—to the shower for having gotten into a heated argument with his black cellmate. Because the officer's charge was rotating his wrists as if he were trying to get out of his handcuffs, the officer lifted him up and threw him facedown into concrete, splitting his skull. Blood shot out of the inmate's head, his nose, and his mouth. I saw this with my own eyes. Black inmates nearby started laughing, which pissed me off. I went to my cell door and screamed:

"What the fuck are y'all laughing at? Because he white? What he do to him he'll do to y'all. He turned blue just like y'all will." If I had been introduced to prison life then and there, I don't know what would have become of me.

"WHICH ONE OF YOU IS MANUEL?" THE muscular black deputy in white shirt and green slacks with a black stripe running down the leg asked as he looked into the holding cell. There were only two of us in it: Cedric from Tampa Park and me. Even two decades later I recognized Cedric from my childhood days in Central Park. Back then he was tall for his age, slim, light-skinned, a pretty boy with deep waves who was popular with girls. Now he was in a holding cell awaiting an evidentiary hearing seeking DNA testing for an offense he swore he didn't commit. I, a thirty-four-year-old man who had spent twenty-one years in prison, was about to witness a courtroom battle between EJI and the state of Florida to determine whether

I was a redeemable human being (deserving of a future) who had made amends for a nonhomicide crime he had committed as a thirteen-year-old child. In short, on December 9, 2011, I was in Tampa yet again for a resentencing hearing during Christmas season, this time to learn how the **Graham** case affected my own.

"Good luck, boy," Cedric said.

" 'Preciate it." I nodded.

The deputy escorted me to the courtroom. I shuffled in my shackles past a window to the right offering a view of downtown Tampa, where I had committed my offense, and a fire department where, as an excited and frightened six-year-old, I had slid down the pole on a school visit. A vision snapped me out of my reverie: I recognized the judge who had presided at my failed hearing in 2000, William Fuente, darting out of one room and into another. As I entered the courtroom, I saw—in addition to my EJI attorneys, Tatiana Bertsch and Ben Schaefer—Aunt Kathy and Lynn, my mother's closest friends, and "Cousin" Anthony there to lend support. There, too, was Debbie Baigrie, with whom

I had been out of touch for more than a decade. Tatiana and Ben had reached out to her, and she had agreed to be present. As Tatiana would later put it to the judge: "[Debbie] did want us to relay to you that she is in support of Mr. Manuel's immediate release with the understanding that his immediate release isn't possible today because he is serving the forty-year sentence and that will remain after today."

"All rise,"[1] the bailiff shouted, as Judge William Fuente emerged from his chamber. Tatiana made a valiant case on my behalf, accounting for my troubled childhood and tumultuous decades of imprisonment and, most important, the progress I had made (how I welcome structure and consistency): "Mr. Manuel sort of defies what the prediction might be for someone who has been in isolation for that long because he has responded so well. And he is—in terms of a window of how he would do transitioning into the free world, his transition into open population has been tremendously positive. He has also received some recognition for his writing. He writes poetry, and he's gotten two certificates at the prison for his writing and was also asked to read a poem. Recently, he received a certificate for organizing a basketball league at the prison—sort of a league; but yes, organizing the team activities. He is very, very interested in pursuing his education upon release, and we are in a position to support that."

I spoke up for myself by reading from a prepared statement: "Your Honor, I sit before you today as a grown man and respectfully request my release. I served twenty-one consecutive years for crimes that I wish were never committed. It is my hope that you reach the conclusion that retribution has been served not just in years of incarceration but in losses incurred during this painful experience, the loss of my mother, brother, father, grandmothers, and every immediate family member I had. But through it all I never lost the audacity of hope or the ability to dream and continue to cling to faith as microscopic as a mustard seed that I must one day be free. My sitting before you today under these miraculous circumstances is fruition of that faith. It's not too late for me to be what I might have been, Your Honor. I ask for the opportunity to become it."

For his part, representing Florida, Assistant State Attorney Thomas Dickerhoof sought to paint me as a hopeless sociopath who at thirteen had been diagnosed with antisocial personality disorder, a diagnosis that still obtained, as he would have it: "According to the DSM-IV, the symptoms of antisocial personality disorder include long-standing pattern of disregard for the rights of others. There is a failure to conform to society's norms and expectations that often results in numerous arrests for legal involvement as well as a history of deceitfulness where the individual attempts to con people or use trickery for personal property. Impulsiveness is often present, including angry outbursts, failure to consider consequences of behavior, irritability, and/or physical assault, all of which he's demonstrated while he's been incarcerated in prison." Dickerhoof argued for a seventy-five-year sentence to run consecutively with the forty years I was already serving, which meant that with full credit for "gain time" I had already earned and would continue to earn, I would be released in thirteen years. Tatiana argued for twenty-seven to forty years to run concurrently with the sentence I was serving, which with "gain time" would have resulted in a much earlier release date.

After listening to Tatiana's declaration that my "remorse is also part of healthy maturation," Judge Fuente looked down at her and said something that led me to believe I would not be going home anytime soon: "You all know even back in 1990 pursuant to Chapter 921 the Legislature told Courts that the primary purpose of sentencing is to punish, not to rehabilitate." With that he disappeared into his chamber. While he was gone Tatiana, Ben, and I talked legal strategy. I wanted to know whether EJI would appeal any sentence that was excessive. I told Tatiana and Ben I didn't think Judge Fuente would announce a consecutive sentence because I thought I heard him cite a precedent. They advised me not to be so sure. There was a lull among us. I turned to look at Debbie. I saw compassion in her eyes.

After a half hour or so, Judge Fuente emerged from his chamber and got right down to business: "I've taken all these matters [comments of counsel, comments of Mr. Manuel, the Defense Counsel's social worker report, the State's Sentencing Memorandum, the 1991 Presentence Investigation, his psychological assessment before sentencing, etc.] into consideration. So the sentence will be as follows. Mr. Manuel, I'll sentence you to sixty-five years in Florida State Prison. Each count to be served concurrently with the other. Each sentence to be followed by two years of community control. Each sentence to be followed by ten years of probation. All standard conditions apply. The one special condition is you participate in the PREP program suggested by Defense Counsel. Since the crime happened in 1990 I'll give you twenty-two years credit against these new sentences. He is entitled to an appeal. He has thirty days to do so."

The bailiff grabbed my arm and led me back to the holding cell, where my mind, addled by crushed expectations, dwelled on what had just happened.

. . .

A FEW HOURS LATER I WAS DRIVEN BACK to Falkenburg Road Jail and led directly to my confinement cell in housing unit 1. I grabbed my Walkman and tuned it to Q105 FM. I was half-expecting to hear my current favorite song, "Someone Like You" by Adele—it was in heavy rotation at the time. I sat on my bunk and started frantically jotting down notes to discuss with my legal team, who had promised to stop by that evening before heading back to Alabama.

"Manuel!" I heard my name called from the intercom in the cell.

"Yeah."

"Get dressed, you got a pro visit."

A pro visit simply meant a legal visit. As I stood up the first chords of the song I had been waiting for came on. "I heard that you're settled down." I scribbled the lyrics of "Someone Like You" on my legal pad and waited for my escort. Falkenburg Road Jail is huge. It's larger than any prison I've been held in. At no other prison did you need a golf cart to get around. The deputy soon arrived to chain and shackle me up. Once we exited the quad he loaded me onto the back of a caged golf cart and drove toward the legal visiting area at the front of the jail. Tatiana, Ben, and Maria had already assembled in a tiny room. Tatiana, whom I now called Ta-Ta, told me that, according to her calculations, my sixty-five-year sentence with credit for gain time for good behavior meant that I would be out in seven or eight years. I was not good at math, but I knew she was being wildly optimistic. All the same, I appreciated her trying to keep my spirits up. I went through my list of issues to raise, possible grounds for appeal.

"The judge sentenced me to sixty-five years for both the robbery and attempted murder. The max he could give me for the attempted murder was forty years. So is my new sentence illegal?"

"Are you sure, Ian?" Tatiana asked. "I thought I heard him say forty."

"Yes, I'm sure. He was so anxious to railroad me he messed up again."

"We'll take a look when we get the transcripts. But if that's accurate that's definitely grounds for a reversal."

We had talked for about an hour when Tatiana reached across the table and pointed to an item on my list I had not discussed and had crossed out, the lyrics of "Someone Like You."

"Ian, are you a fan?" I couldn't quite make out her tone.

I glanced at Maria and asked if she had remembered to bring Adele's **21** CD, which I had begged her for, and the pair of Nike Air Max shoes that Mrs. Cooper, an old Christian lady, had sent after reading about me in the newspaper and that I had never gotten to wear. I must have assumed when I made my request that after the hearing I would be leaving with everyone for Alabama.

"Yes, it and the shoes."

The seemingly ordinary exchange slammed me to the core. I felt the full impact of the demolition of my dream of early release. And I did something I don't do. I cried. Full of compassion, Maria wrapped her arms around me as I sobbed. She whispered:

"It's different this time, Ian."

She was reassuring me I was not alone as I had been in 2000, when I was fighting for my freedom on my own. I now had a team of dedicated EJI lawyers standing by me—and a social worker who loved and cared for me unconditionally.

"Yes, but it hurts more this time, Maria."

I cried on her shoulder for several minutes. Then we separated and sat back down. I wiped my eyes and regained my composure. I could see pain in Tatiana's and Ben's eyes but no tears. They were being strong for me. We said our goodbyes; they all promised to be in touch before Christmas.

A week later I was chained and loaded into a van in the early morning hours. I was returning to Suwannee to start my sixty-five-year sentence. Once the garage door opened we drove quickly away from the jail and were on the highway in no time. I lowered my head and squinted through the small oval openings of an iron panel. I stared at the Tampa skyline and landscape as they receded. I was entranced: I imagined Judge Fuente's face as these "Someone Like You" lyrics popped into my head: "I hate to turn up out of the blue, uninvited/But I couldn't stay away, I couldn't fight it/I had hoped you'd see my face/And that you'd be reminded that for me, it isn't over . . . /'Don't forget me,' I beg . . . /'Sometimes it lasts in love but sometimes it hurts instead.'"

"I'll be back," I muttered.

My sadness turned to anger and determination as we drove beyond the city limits. I didn't know how and I didn't know when I would return, but I was certain in my soul that Tampa had not seen the last of me.

11

RIGHT BEFORE CHRISTMAS 2011, WHEN I returned to Suwannee crushed by not having been set free at my resentencing hearing, as I had all too unreasonably expected, my anger was tempered by the festive aura of the holiday season. I was beginning to come to terms with how arduous the legal fight for my freedom would be, and was looking forward to Ben and Maria's visit. Things were going fine—as fine as they can be in open population. I had money in my account, sent to me by strangers while I was in Tampa's county jail, and had amassed even more right after I returned to Suwannee when I won a football pool. I was feeling lucky. One day I was sitting in P dorm playing poker with a few of the guys, even though I am as terrible a poker player as they come because I can't hide my emotions. Over the intercom I heard my name. You receive a "call out" when you must report to a medical, dental, or mental health appointment or when you have classification issues or business in the property room. When I got up to cash in my chips I realized that I didn't have any.

I walked out the dormitory door toward the gate, and standing there was Sergeant O'Shea, the gang sergeant, a short—five foot four or so—blond woman with a reputation for planting knives on inmates and locking them up for nothing. If you knew what was good for you, you'd stay clear of her. I knew as much, and yet . . .

"You seen me coming, why'd you close the gate?"

"What? Who are you talking to?"

"I'm talking to you." My instinctual response was crazy; I should have gone out of my way not to mess with this lady, but I couldn't help it—and I should have been able to, given the stakes. Did I have it in me to comport myself so as to avoid ever being on close management again? The gate was remotely popped and as I walked through she addressed me.

"You keep mouthing off like that, Manuel, and you're gonna have to report to my office."

"Well, shit, let's head there right now." This was all on me, and it was not going to end well.

"Turn around," she ordered.

"Turn around? For what?"

"You goin' to jail, you just threatened me."

She puts a hand on her Mace canister. If I say or do anything that might result in her gassing me, she will justify it by saying I assaulted her—and that will send me immediately back to CM. We're standing near the gun tower and, of course, cameras are trained on us. I turn around; she handcuffs me. She will still have to fabricate an excuse for forcing me once again into confinement, but now I am solely responsible for the predicament in which I find myself.

She escorts me to the back door of medical and stops. I had stared at her with all of the pent-up anger that had been simmering in me for more than a week, since my resentencing. She is clearly terrified by the look on my face, and she presses the panic button on her walkie-talkie. Officers come running from all over the compound to assist her.

"You were gonna jump me when I opened the door, weren't you?"

"What's wrong with you, lady? I'm handcuffed."

Her boyfriend, another sergeant, grabs me and drags me to a holding cell. After they uncuff me, I slice my arm with the razor I keep in my possession everywhere I go. While I'm in medical, the sergeant and her beau visit my cell and rifle through my things, flinging them around. They find letters from Maria on EJI stationery with her standard sign-off, "Love, Maria." They accuse Maria of conducting an unprofessional relationship with me and ban her from visiting me for more than a year and a half.

My cutting myself triggers routine procedures. I am at once bored and transfixed by their sameness. I am hauled off to Suwannee's crisis stabilization unit (CSU) for a spell, and something unexpected changes my life. It is early morning one weekend. Officers like to come through raging at the crack of dawn while inmates are asleep, but I'm an early bird and already up. To make life easy for themselves, they try to dissuade you from going to the dayroom, which is your right, by putting you in chains and shackling you before leading you there. Sometimes, to add to your anxiety, they search your cell while you're away, and you never know what they might find or plant. They want you to be as miserable as possible, and that is why the dayroom television set features only PBS programming, as opposed to the sports and entertainment shows that inmates love to watch.

The hour-long documentary playing that day—intended as a form of correctional punishment—enthralled me. It was called **To Be Heard** and had won a bunch of awards. It was about three teenagers from the South Bronx struggling to change their lives through devotion to writing and reciting poetry as self-expression—poetry of frustration and hope, love and friendship, among other vicissitudes of life. A powerful bond formed among them as they strove to address the circumstances of their lives through language. These teens—Anthony, a slim, thick-lipped young man full of energy who reminded me of Jay-Z; Pearl, a stout, strong, soulful black girl; and Karina, passionate and good-hearted and of mixed racial heritage—rocked me deeply. I had been writing poetry as a means to cope, a form of therapy, but I had never been exposed to the sheer force of power poetry, slam poetry.

I was so inspired by what I had seen and heard that I couldn't wait to get back to my cell to try this new medium out. I put pen to paper, and the result was a poem I called "Every Time I Breathe," about valuing and enjoying life. The next week I shared my efforts at a group therapy session with other inmates. Their response was highly encouraging. I recall our counselor saying that the poem should be read in every crisis stabilization and transition care unit in the state of Florida.

EVERY TIME I BREATHE

Every time I breathe I feel the need to
    justify my existence
To take this moment that I'm living
    and enjoy every millisecond in it
My life and my struggles not many
    can comprehend it.
My desire for freedom burns like a
    sausage in a skillet
Tomorrow isn't promised so I'm
    thankful for this minute.
Though imprisoned merely existing
    it's like my life has been suspended.
But that means it's temporary because
    I haven't been expelled.
And I still got a chance as long as I
    can in and exhale.
Every time I breathe.
Every time I breathe I'm thankful for
    the oxygen from the trees.
And little things like little bees that
    get overlooked until they sting.
Everyday I'm faced with obstacles that
    block the progress to my dreams.

But the blockades are only
    masquerades like costumes
    on halloween.
I've been through enough pain to
    make a sane man just scream.
But instead I take a deep breath and
    just breathe.
Every time I breathe the cosmos come
    out of my nostrils.
Like particles of Prada coming out of
    your console.
My soul is like a chihuahua you didn't
    include in your carpool
My lungs relax and collapse like a
    bottom sitting on a bar stool.
Every time I breathe.
Every time I breathe I become an
    intergalactic being.
Stepping out of character like a
    chiropractor snapping peas.
I've prayed so many times it's like I've
    got arthritis in my knees.
But I still get down and bow my head
    because I continue to believe.
That as long as I can breathe God's
    going to make a change.

And my circumstances are only
  chances for me to glorify his name.
You don't know me homie. But there's
  odds I've already overcame.
So if praying works. But hurts. Then I
  can stand a little pain.
I want to end this part by thanking
  God for bringing me to
  these heights.
And I make a promise to always
  honor and cherish this breath
  of life.
Every time I breathe. Every time I
  breathe. Every time I breathe!

. . .

BECAUSE SUWANNEE LACKED A TRANSI-tional care unit, I was shipped off again to Lake Correctional Institution. There my worst fears were realized: I was confronted with disciplinary reports that Sergeant O'Shea had made up, requiring time in confinement—perhaps even CM—on my return to Suwannee. I was ashamed that I had put myself in this position. If I had only . . . Maria called to embolden me: "Ian, you can't run from this. You have to face it." While at Lake, I received a visit out of the blue from the former warden at Santa Rosa who had arranged for me to be transferred to Suwannee. He was now a regional director in the Department of Corrections.

"Manuel, God damn you. I got you off CM and now I hear you're trying to get back."

"No, sir, I ain't. I'll be honest with you. When I first got to Suwannee, things were fine. I was doing good. I was in the rec department; I was the basketball commissioner. I learned how to lead—how as a leader you have to delegate authority to people who are better than you at certain things for your team to succeed. But then that new warden came in and turned that place upside down. He turned it into a hellhole."

"So what now? What you want?"

"Man, I wanna go to one of them private institutions. Graceville or South Bay."

"No, I don't think that will be happening. I'm keeping you right here in Region Three with me."

"In that case, you remember when we had that conversation at Santa Rosa and you told me I wouldn't like Charlotte and you sent me to Suwannee instead? Well, how 'bout Charlotte?"

"Wherever I send you, the warden will come talk to you. Just be patient."

IT WAS TIME TO RETURN TO SUWANNEE TO face the music—to deal with the lies Sergeant O'Shea had told about me in her disciplinary reports, lies about how I had threatened or even attacked her. Given my conversation with the regional director, however, I was not expecting to remain at the institution for long, much less to be placed on close management. All the same, you never know. It would be untrue to say I wasn't worried. At the time,

all forms of confinement at Suwannee—
administrative, disciplinary, or CM—were
savage, the difference being only a matter of
degree. On the most basic level, the cells were
freezing, sometimes in the fifties; your food
tray was flung into your cell, splattering the
walls; and then, of course, there was the infamous 5:00 a.m. to 5:00 p.m. rule. When I
met with the warden and Sergeant O'Shea,
one of them said (I don't remember which):

"Manuel, if I wanted to, I could fuck you
up, send you back to CM, starve you to death,
but I don't want none of that. I want my confinement time. I want my ninety days."

I was placed not in CM but in open population confinement for disciplinary reasons.
In open population, you leave your cell for
breakfast, lunch, and dinner; in open population confinement, you eat all meals in your
cell. In open population, you can go to call
outs without being handcuffed or shackled;
in open population confinement, you cannot.
In two weeks during those ninety days, I furiously wrote down my life story to age fifteen
and called it **Inside/Out.** The other nineteen
years were too painful to contemplate.

The transactional nature of life behind bars—between the Department of Corrections and correctional facilities, wardens and guards, guards and inmates, and among inmates themselves—informs this demand. Why did authorities of a facility renowned for its brutishness all of a sudden want "none of that"? What was in it for them? What transaction—about which I was in the dark—had taken place between them and perhaps the regional director? I was released to open population in June 2012.

A sergeant working L dorm remembered me from when she was an officer at Union Correctional Institution and shared a perception of me as a troublemaker. One night when she was doing count, I violated procedure. I think she caught me talking and called me out. She called for help and yet again I was put in confinement, where I proceeded yet again to cut myself. I spent the night in a suicide observation cell. The next day the captain who ran the ship was making his rounds and stopped by.

"Listen, man, a couple things—don't be giving my officers no problem. I need you to stay calm. I've got two inmates in here for assault on officers and I'm getting ready to gas 'em. I need you to stay out of my business. Don't be hollering and carrying on as you always do when we do what we gotta do."

"OK, but I'm gonna need something from you. When I get out from this cage I'll need a move."

"A move? That's it? No problem."

The captain walked away. That night, as I tried to sleep, I heard screams and smelled the gas. It smelled of oranges; I knew it burned skin like hot peppers in your mouth.

IN L DORM THERE WAS A MAN NAMED Joshua; his boyfriend slept in O dorm. They often met furtively at the medication window at noon to spend a little time together. Joshua was permitted to be there but not his partner, and so they sometimes were written up for "corrective consultation"—less than a disciplinary report. Joshua became frustrated and said to me:

"Ian, I'm tired of this shit. I wish I could get a move on."

"I can get that done; but you're gonna have to pay."

"How much?"

"Fifty dollars."

A formal request to move from one dorm to another involved filling out a slip that was never answered or was denied. I stood to make good money if I could move Joshua's partner to his dorm. I approached the captain who, when I was in confinement, had promised me a move.

"Look, I'll do this move for you," he told me. "I know who you're talking about; he a gang member. If I move him to L dorm and he starts any bullshit, I'm gonna gas you and do you worse than you've ever been done."

"Cool."

The captain moved Joshua's boyfriend; Joshua couldn't believe it.

Neither could I. I had gone from being unable to move, stuck inside a box and denied any human interaction, to being able to move others. I had become a businessman, and I was stunned to find myself in a position to help others while supporting myself. The more transactions I made, the more resentment grew among some inmates. Gangbangers threatened to snitch if I didn't give them a piece of the action. Others claimed that I myself was doing the snitching—why else would the nastiest captain on the compound be favoring me? What they didn't know was that, in essence, the captain was moving people for me in exchange for me keeping things calm and hassle-free for his officers. I had become a part of the DOC's corrupt system of management.

The captain was a good ol' boy. Even though he was under scrutiny, there was no tangible proof against him. I wasn't about to provide that proof, even though when he was not helping me out he was gassing and beating inmates. Prison is complicated, transactional. I don't know what eventually happened to him. Me? In the dead of night I was transferred to Charlotte Correctional Institution.

FOR YEARS I HAD BELIEVED THAT INCARceration at Charlotte was more desirable than elsewhere—I had heard it on the grapevine. On the bright side, Maria was allowed to visit me for the first time in a year and a half. She came with Ben and Tatiana for a legal and social visit, at the end of which Maria asked whether I had noticed anything different about her.

"Did you gain a little weight?"

"Ian, I'm pregnant."

I had never given much thought to Maria's life outside of our friendship and her devotion to my case, yet this development somehow made me feel insecure, vulnerable to abandonment. All the same, I was struck by how happy she looked and congratulated her. On the dark side of Charlotte in 2013, I was remanded to close management for the first time since 2010 and, because Charlotte did not have a CM program, I was sent back to Santa Rosa to satisfy the order. Whatever hope of freedom I may have been harboring collapsed.

I did the ninety days of good behavior at Santa Rosa and, as has happened time and again, the rug was pulled from under my feet.

"Ian, you've done so well; we can tell you're a different man now. We're going to put you on CM 3 with a ninety-day review. Behave yourself for ninety days more, and you're back in open population. It don't get no sweeter than that."

I shudder when I hear this; I worry that in those three months something within or beyond my control will happen, resulting in a DR that will put me back on the CM treadmill—and sure enough, something does. I don't like going to the dayroom here to watch TV because they strip you naked before they take you, but one day I ask to go. Officers come to my cell, shout bullshit that I have not made my bed correctly, and deny me my privilege. I am beside myself with fury; they gas me with their canisters. An inmate in such a circumstance must be gassed only if he is trying to hurt himself. I am not. The punishment I receive is gratuitous, and that is why I am not charged with a disciplinary report. I remain on CM 3. I confide to a mental health counselor that I have been gassed for no reason, that I will ask my lawyers to investigate the incident and shut this kind of shit down. She advises me not to be so threatening.

In December I am issued a falsified disciplinary report for having threatened correctional officers. It says officers came to my cell to take me to shower and I stated: "If you open that door, I'm going to kick Officer such-and-such's ass." Make up whatever name you wish, because it was a lie. One month before I am to be released to open population—and based on a lie—I am forced to regress from CM 3 to CM 2. I am subjected to heightened security. Whenever I must leave my cell for whatever reason, I must back out and kneel immediately to be handcuffed and shackled.

In the wake of my 2011 resentencing hearing, this was one of the grimmest periods of my life, among the hardest for me to reckon with, when time just seemed like an abyss in which I was falling endlessly, even as I clung to the tenuous belief that there had to be a divine rationale for my suffering and pain, and that someday I would walk out of prison a free man.

HERE, IN THE FULL GLORY OF ITS PERVER-sity, is the legal madness pertaining to time that I had been dealing with. On April 11, 1991, when I was fourteen years old I was sentenced to "natural life" on count one (attempted armed robbery); fifteen years in prison on count two (attempted robbery); life without parole on count three (attempted murder in the first degree with a firearm); and life probation on count four (attempted murder with a firearm). The sentences for counts one, two, and three were to run concurrently, while the sentence for count four was to obtain, in effect, after "natural life."

On April 17, 2000, the court partly denied and partly granted my motion to correct this sentence. It found that my initial sentence of two terms of life followed by life probation was beyond guidelines. On June 29, 2000, the court resentenced me, on count four only, to forty years to run concurrently with the sentences for counts one, two, and three— ensuring that my debt to society would be settled at the expiration of my life without parole sentence, meaning at the expiration of my life.

In the wake of the U.S. Supreme Court's ruling on **Graham v. Florida** in 2010—stipulating that "for a juvenile offender who did not commit homicide the Eighth Amendment forbids the sentence of life without parole"— the court, on December 9, 2011, resentenced me, for counts one and three, to sixty-five years in prison, plus two years of community control and eight years of probation, to run concurrently with the sentences for counts two and four. Directly after this hearing, in early 2012, my EJI lawyers filed on my behalf a motion to correct the sentence on counts one and three—based on the **Graham** decision and because the maximum allowable sentence for a life felony, according to Florida statutes, is either forty years in prison or a life sentence. The court denied me relief for count one (sixty-five years for attempted robbery) but resentenced me for count three to forty years instead of the previous sixty-five. This minor victory was a cosmic joke.

FOR FORTY DAYS AND FORTY NIGHTS I WAS on death row—actually, underneath death row—and it helped me to understand how sacred life is, and that there were conditions even worse than mine. I had been transferred to Florida State Prison in September 2014 to serve the rest of my CM 3 time in a confinement wing below death row. I was looking forward to being released yet again to open population; inmates on death row were anticipating, whether imminent or not, their inevitable annihilation by the state. Their hopelessness had a pure authenticity about it. Yet you learn that death row inmates are granted privileges that you are not; they can, for example, order tobacco products—and in prison tobacco as a commodity is king. One day, together with other inmates, I was taken to the exercise cage in the yard. While doing pull-ups on a bar, I realized I was exercising next to the death chamber, where they strap you down and kill you. There was a window draped with white; I couldn't see through it. But being in such close proximity to the killing room does something to you; it alters you in an unexpected way; it compels you to appreciate life in full. And my association with death row inmates made me understand deep in my bones something that I was unable to articulate at the time but that is captured in Bryan Stevenson's **Just Mercy:**

"Each of us is more than the worst thing we've ever done."

Dontae Morris, father of a seven-year-old, shot and killed five human beings, including two police officers in Tampa between May and July 2010. For his crimes he was at first sentenced to life imprisonment but subsequently was sentenced to death three times. This notorious cold-blooded murderer, a reputed member of the Bloods gang, was supposedly a man without a conscience. But when I arrived at Florida State, he showed me empathy, even though by then prison had made him crazier than he probably was otherwise. One of the prison runarounds told me that Dontae was right above me. I got on the vent and yelled upstairs:

"Hey, Dontae, Dontae: check this out, this here's Jim-Jim from Central Park. I know you might not know me, man, but I just got here from Santa Rosa and I ain't got a lot of property. Soon as I get my property I'll be straight. I need you to let me borrow some stamps, envelopes, writing paper, and something to eat, until I get my property."

"All right I got you, man, what cell you in?"

Dontae arranged for his minions to provide for me without expecting anything in return. I learned a lot from his kindness: even Dontae Morris—deemed most contemptible and irredeemable among us—was capable of a simple act of decency.

ON NOVEMBER 19, 2014, EJI FILED ANOTHER motion to correct sentence—sixty-five years for count one (robbery)—based on the resolution of a case that seems in retrospect to have been a serendipitous godsend. Who knows what my fate might have been without it? I felt that **Peters v. State**[1] represented some kind of cosmic realignment in my life. As Maria had said, this time it was different. Now I was convinced—I had substantive legal reason to believe—that, finally, my time would come, and the state of Florida would have no grounds for appeal. Roughly a year earlier, Florida's Fourth District Court of Appeal had published a ruling that was especially germane to my situation.

The **Peters** court was obliged to take the U.S. Supreme Court's **Graham** decision—which held that the Eighth Amendment's cruel and unusual punishment clause prohibits juveniles from being sentenced to life in prison without parole for a nonhomicide offense—into consideration when it reviewed a juvenile sentence for a first-degree felony punishable by life. It found that a sentence of more than forty years in prison for a first-degree felony was unconstitutionally disproportionate because a similarly situated juvenile convicted of a life felony could receive a sentence of no more than forty years in accordance with statutory language between October 1, 1983, and July 1, 1995. Thus **Peters v. State** determined that a more severe sentence for a less serious offense is an affront to the Constitution. As a result of this "statutory anomaly," it concluded that "juvenile defendants convicted of aggravated first degree felonies committed between October 1, 1983, and July 1, 1995, may not be sentenced beyond forty years imprisonment." This meant that if the court reviewing EJI's "motion to correct sentence" were to rule in my favor, I would have to be released from prison imminently, because of time I had already served plus "gain time."[2]

In August 2015, a judge in the Thirteenth Judicial Circuit Court could not hide his displeasure at having to rule by the book in my favor:[3]

After reviewing defendant's motion, the state's response, defendant's reply, the court file, and the record, the court vehemently disagrees with reasoning of the **Peters** court in reaching its specific holding regarding limitations on sentencing juveniles for first degree felonies punishable by life. Yet, consistent with its oath, this court finds that it is bound to follow the existing and binding case law from the Fourth District Court of Appeal . . . The court notes its belief that the Second District Court of Appeal would likely decide this issue differently and thus the issue is ripe for the Second District Court of Appeal to rule upon any appeal of this ruling and certify conflict to the Florida Supreme Court.

Here was the state of Florida—and a judge to boot—suggesting, a quarter century after my nonhomicide crime and imprisonment, that a law its own judicial system had handed down, a law that would set me free, should be proscribed. Confidently optimistic though I may have been, I was not entirely out of the woods yet. In August 2016 the Second District Court handed down its decision: "We agree with **Peters** that it requires Manuel to be resentenced to no more than forty years in prison on the 1990 offense of robbery with a firearm in count one due to the statutory anomaly. Thus we affirm the trial court's order." Coming when it did, the ruling meant that I had been given an extra year of prison time on the house.

ON NOVEMBER 10, 2016—TWO DAYS AFTER Donald J. Trump was elected president of the United States—I was back in Tampa to be resentenced as the Second District Court had stipulated. That morning in Hillsborough Circuit Court Annex, my EJI family, Ben Schaefer and Maria Morrison, and members of my extended family—my mother's friends Aunt Kathy and Aunt Lynn—were there to support me. So too, with grace, was Debbie

Baigrie, a victim of the crime I had committed twenty-six years earlier. I had not seen Debbie since 2011 and had not communicated with her in more than a decade, but she had been in frequent contact with my legal team and had agreed to attend the hearing in support of my release. Now thirty-nine years old and having spent two-thirds of my life in prison, I stood before a man I had regarded as my nemesis for sixteen years, the Honorable William Fuente, who on two previous occasions, in 2000 and 2011, had frustrated my motions to correct sentence. His tone, however, was different this time, warmer, sympathetic:

"Well, as you know, the law has changed dramatically since the early nineties, when you were before the court originally, and today the law requires a much more different attitude and view toward juveniles. Be that as it may, the crimes can still be serious. In any event, in keeping with the—in accordance with I guess the mandate from the Second DCA . . . I'll vacate the most recently imposed sentence in count one, which I think this court imposed, which was sixty-five years FSP followed by two years community control, followed by eight years of probation. And at this time I'll resentence Mr. Manuel to forty years Florida State Prison to be served concurrently with all other counts with credit for all time served, including any earned gain time that he may have gained with the Department of Corrections . . . And that essentially—that probably puts him in fairly close to release, doesn't it?"[4]

"Thank you, Jesus, thank you, Jesus," Aunt Kathy screamed, piercing the fleeting silence in the courtroom. As raucous jubilation broke out around me, I was stunned, for a moment not knowing what to think. Was my ordeal finally over? The world was all before me now, but what exactly did that mean?

That night at around 9:30, as I walked out of Orange County Jail in prison garb, carrying the barest of possessions in a bag, Maria rushed past Ben, Aunt Lynn, and Lynn's grown son, who were there as well to greet me. She embraced me and spun me around and gave me clothes—a red shirt and jeans—and the pair of unworn Air Maxes she and I had agreed I would wear whenever I was released. After I had changed and thanked

Aunt Lynn and her son before bidding them goodbye, Maria, Ben, and I proceeded to a gas station just down the street from the jail. It had been agreed that Debbie would meet us there. She and I stared at each other and grinned before hugging. Ben was busy trying to figure out where we would eat; we were all starving. He settled on a pizza joint downtown, not realizing that it was ever so close to where I had shot Debbie a quarter century before. When I got out of the car, I grabbed Debbie and kissed her on both cheeks to acknowledge the disaster that brought us into each other's life. I ate pizza greedily, devouring my own and sampling everybody's. The wall behind us featured a framed picture of the Brooklyn Bridge.

That night, Ben, Maria, and I drove out of Tampa on the first leg of our trek to Alabama, where I would enroll in EJI's reentry program to reacquaint myself with the rudiments of life in society. Dozing on and off in the backseat of the car, I reflected on the statement I had read before Judge Fuente in court:

"I stand before you today, Your Honor, against all judicial odds. It is rare and improbable for someone with my particular set of circumstances to be standing before you again to be resentenced for the fourth time for a sentence determined to be illegal and unconstitutional. Initially, I was a child sentenced to die in prison, an adolescent full of aspirations, cast into this vast ocean filled with adult sharks and predators and told to swim, survive, find my way back to shore the best way I could. Well, here I am, but I'm not unscathed by my journey. My heart bears the pain of my punishment. Look around this courtroom, it is different. The faces have changed from the original cast members. The Judge, the State, the Defense, my mom, dad, brother, et cetera, everybody except Debbie and me, two people with one common interest waiting on the justice system to catch up with my remorse and her forgiveness. Hopefully, today is the day we can stand together as an example, in a country deeply divided by so many racial dimensions, that justice does prevail, that wrongs will be made right [and that as] English Lit teaches us, all sentences have a period that brings them to an end."

Acknowledgments

First and foremost, I'd like to thank God for making all of this possible.

To my editor, Erroll McDonald. To my agents Peter and Amy Bernstein.

To Maria Morrison, Tom and Andi Bernstein, Charlotte Morrison, Ben Schaefer, Meg Laughlin, Martha Elliot, Lynn Creal, Kathy Miller, Anthony Baker, Lili Lynton, Jason Flom, Bob Gilbertson, and to a host of others responsible for the man I am today.

Notes

CHAPTER 3

1. Debbie Baigrie, as told to Roul Tunley, "I Forgave the Guy Who Shot Me," **McCall's,** September 1996, 54.
2. **The Tampa Tribune,** Wednesday, August 22, 1990, 14.
3. Baigrie, Debbie, as told to Tunley, Roul, "I Forgave the Guy Who Shot Me," **McCall's,** September 1996, 56.
4. The following re-creation comes from the transcript of: State of Florida v. Ian Manuel, 90-12780, RPR-CP (13th Cir. 1991).
5. Hillary Clinton, "superpredators" (speech, Keene State College, NH, January 28, 1996), https:/www.youtube.com/watch?v=j0uCrA7ePno.
6. State of Florida v. Ian Manuel.
7. Ibid.

CHAPTER 4

1. Bryan A. Stevenson, "Cruel and Unusual: Sentencing 13- and 14-Year-Old Children to Die in Prison" **Current Issues in Criminal Justice** 20, no. 1 (2008): 135–140. https://doi.org/10.1080/10345329.2008.12056193.
2. Proverbs 30: 24–28 (New International Version).

CHAPTER 5

1. Amy Roe, "Solitary Confinement Is Especially Harmful to Juveniles and Should Not Be Used to Punish Them," **ACLU Washington,** November 17, 2017, https://www.aclu-wa.org/story/solitary-confinement-especially-harmful-juveniles-and-should-not-be-used-punish-them.

CHAPTER 6

1. Mary Hawthorne, "Charles Dickens on Solitary Confinement," **New Yorker,** March 23, 2009, https://www.newyorker.com/books/page-turner/dept-of-amplification-charles-dickens-on-solitary-confinement.
2. Ibid.
3. Fla. Admin. Code R. 8H-3.02, 33-601.800 Close Management.

4. John J. Dilulio, **Body Count** (New York: Simon & Schuster, 1996), 27.

5. Debbie Baigrie, as told to Roul Tunley, "I Forgave the Guy Who Shot Me," **McCall's,** September 1996.

6. Following quotes come from State of Florida v. Ian Manuel, 90-12780, (13th Cir. 2000).

CHAPTER 7

1. Osterback v. McDonough, 549 F. Supp. 2d 1337 (M.D. Fla. 2008).

2. Meg Laughlin, "Does Separation Equal Suffering?" **Tampa Bay Times,** August 25, 2007.

CHAPTER 8

1. Deborah Brodsky and Cyrus O'Brien, "No Place for a Child: Direct File of Juveniles Comes at a High Cost; Time to Fix Statutes," James Madison Institute, February 2016.

2. Bryan A. Stevenson, **Just Mercy** (New York: One World, 2014).

3. **LockUp,** "Inside Florida and Santa Rosa Prison," MSNBC.

CHAPTER 9

1. Roper v. Simmons, 543 U.S. 551 (2005).

2. Adam Liptak, "Defining 'Cruel and Unusual'

When Offender Is 13," **New York Times,** February 2, 2009.

3. Sullivan v. Florida 560 U.S. 181 (2010).
4. Meg Laughlin, "In Ian's World," **Tampa Bay Times,** May 17, 2010.
5. "Imprisoning a Child for Life," **New York Times,** November 9, 2009, 22.
6. Sullivan v. Florida 560 U.S. 181 (2010).
7. Graham v. Florida 560 U.S. 48 (2010).
8. Ibid.

CHAPTER 10

1. State of Florida v. Ian Manuel, 90-CF-12780, TD-2 (13th Cir. 2011).

CHAPTER 11

1. Peters v. State, 919 So.2d 624, 628 (Fla. 1st DCA 2006).
2. Florida state law also allows inmates to accumulate "gain time," by which they can shave ten days off their sentences per month. Inmates can earn gain time by things including good behavior, education, and educational achievement.
3. State of Florida v. Ian Manuel, 90-CF-12780, TD-2 (13th Cir. 2015).
4. State of Florida v. Ian Manuel, 90-CF-12780, TD-2 (13th Cir. 2016).

Permissions Acknowledgments

Grateful acknowledgment is made to the following for permission to reprint previously published material:

Alfred Music: Lyric excerpt from "Anything for You," words and music by Gloria Estefan. Copyright © 1987 by Foreign Imported Productions & Publishing, Inc. (BMI). All rights reserved. Reprinted by permission of Alfred Music.

Hal Leonard LLC: Lyric excerpt from "Like A Star," words and music by Corinne Bailey Rae. Copyright © 2006 by Global Talent Publishing. All rights administered by Downtown DMP Songs. All rights reserved. · Lyric excerpt from "Someone Like You," words and music by Adele Adkins and Dan Wilson. Copyright © 2011 by Melted Stone Publishing Ltd., BMG Monarch and Sugar Lake Music. All rights for Melted Stone Publishing Ltd. in the U.S. and Canada controlled and administered by Universal—Songs of Polygram International, Inc. All rights for BMG Monarch and Sugar Lake Music administered by BMG Rights Management (US) LLC. All rights reserved. Reprinted by permission of Hal Leonard LLC.

A Note About the Author

IAN MANUEL lives in New York City. He is a motivational speaker at schools and social organizations nationwide.